COGNITIVE BEHAVIORAL THERAPY

Change your Life with easy CBT Techniques and Strategies to Overcome Fear, Panic, Anxiety, Depression, Anger, Worry, Negativity and Intrusive Thoughts

- Jake Nigram –

Legal Notice

Disclaimer Notice:

Please note the information contained within this document is for educational and entertainment purposes only. Every attempt has been made to provide accurate, up to date and reliable complete information. No warranties of any kind are expressed or implied. Readers acknowledge that the author is not engaging in the rendering of legal, financial, medical or professional advice. By reading this document, the reader agrees that under no circumstances are we responsible for any losses, direct or indirect, which are incurred as a result of the use of information contained within this document, including, but not limited to, errors, omissions, or inaccuracies.

TABLE OF CONTENTS

Cognitive Behavioral Teraphy: *Change your Life with easy CBT Techniques and Strategies to Overcome Fear, Panic, Anxiety, Depression, Anger, Worry, Negativity and Intrusive Thoughts*

INTRODUCTION

Cognitive Therapy, when merged with behavioral therapy proves to be more effective than treatment using medication alone. As the individual becomes aware or recognizes his own negative thinking and faulty beliefs as the major causes of his behavioral issue, he starts to think positively. The mere fact that he is conscious of what is happening in him and he intends to make a change is evidence of his positive thinking. This is a major shift from his previous thinking pattern.

Due to CBT goal and action-oriented execution, both the therapist and the person with behavioral disorders collaborate equally in exploring and executing effective techniques which can challenge the individual's thinking and eventually lead to his positive actions. By addressing thoughts, emotions, and behaviors which contribute to the development and maintenance of psychological issues, CBT seeks to offer a holistic approach to mental health care. Simply put, CBT requires two basic activities: learning and doing something based on what you have learned.

Under the CBT umbrella, REBT is likewise an effective approach as the person with the disorder becomes aware that he alone has the responsibility to change his perception of things and situations in response to triggers that challenge his thinking. The treatment is empowered through his choices for the CBT treatment to be successful; the individual must be willing to commit to the treatment of proactive approach and structure. To sum it up, Cognitive Behavioral Therapy can be effective not only for the treatment of various psychological disorders but can likewise help in maintaining mental care through management of stress. Adopting CBT can have its long-term gains but care should be taken in selecting one's therapist.

This guide entails the following:

- Basics of CBT
- Your Thoughts
- Benefits of Treatment CTB
- CBT Therapy
- CBT Advantages and Methods
- CBT For Treatment of Addiction
- Change Your Life for The Better with The CBT

- CBT Strategies for Overcome Your Fear, Panic, Anxiety, Depression, Anger and Worry

- Putting CBT To Practice

- Working on Specifically Anxiety, Negativity, and Stress... AND MORE!!!

Chapter 1: Cognitive Behavioral Therapy (CTB)

What is CBT?

Cognitive behavioral therapy was developed from rational emotive behavioral therapy and cognitive therapy. Rational emotive behavioral therapy was practiced on the idea that many of our negative emotional experiences are created by the thoughts we have around the situations in which they arise, and not necessarily the situations themselves.

This was one of the first forms of therapy that really examined how our thoughts can impact the way we approach situations and handle our emotions. Cognitive therapy focused on addressing the negative thought patterns individuals had about themselves as well as their surroundings. This therapy seeks to change unwanted behaviors and negative emotional states.

Cognitive behavioral therapy combines both these types of therapy. It focuses on addressing the way we think, the emotions we feel, and the resulting behavior that occurs. By focusing on how an individual's thoughts can affect their emotions and cause predictable behaviors, one can begin to change their negative experiences by simply focusing on changing the way they think. When you suffer from severe anxiety, fear, anger, or negative thought patterns, it can be difficult to take the necessary steps on your own to look at things in a more productive and beneficial way.

When you utilize a number of various tools but still find yourself stuck experiencing negative emotions, defaulting to negative thought patterns, and having a negative attitude towards life, therapy can be helpful in understanding and recognizing where and what causes you to fall into the negative process. Cognitive behavioral therapy is a type of talk therapy where you look at issues of the present moment and work to overcome the negative thoughts, behaviors, and emotions that occur in specific situations. This type of psychotherapy uncovers the thoughts, beliefs, and attitudes that can hinder individuals from living fully happy and healthy lives.

Cognitive behavioral therapy is very goal-oriented and problem-specific, meaning the patient and therapist work together to pinpoint specific events, situations, and thoughts that need to be resolved. Realistic and attainable goals are set and action steps are created for the patient to overcome the negative patterns. Through this type of therapy, one can learn to recognize the negative thought patterns which do not serve in helping to resolve situations. This allows you to become more aware of the psychological issues these negative thoughts can cause. It also addresses the behaviors that can cause psychological issues and helps individuals learn more appropriate reactions.

Individuals are also supplied with a variety of tools and processes that will help them form more positive habits and coping skills to resolve the negative thoughts, behaviors, and emotions as opposed to avoiding, suppressing, or hiding from them. Cognitive behavioral therapy has been an effective way for many individuals who suffer from mental health disorders to reclaim their lives. It offers a new way of thinking and a new approach to dealing with difficult situations in the future.

What you learn through the session are techniques and methods that help you shift your negative thoughts to positive ones, and how to apply these techniques in any situation where you feel strong negative emotions. This is done by a process of rewiring and reprogramming the brain to break the cycle of negative patterns and behaviors and put into practice positive and beneficial patterns and behaviors.

Many hesitate to take part in this type of therapy because it is often viewed as superficial and many of the techniques come off as corny, but when you go into cognitive therapy with an open mind and a true desire to improve your life, it can be highly beneficial. This is because of the effect this type of therapy can have on the brain. Through cognitive behavioral therapy, you actually change the ways neurons interact with one another. This change in neuron communication occurs because of the rewiring within these neural networks.

Neural networks are specific lines of communications which are organized into various groups according to topics, themes, thoughts, situations, and emotions. Cognitive therapy helps you first focus attention on a specific network, strengthening certain neuronal bonds while weakening others, which will ultimately result in the loss of neural networks. When you begin to focus your attention on more positive thoughts, you focus on the neural networks associated with those positive thoughts. But these thoughts have to be specific — if you want to think of yourself in a more positive light, you would focus on what exactly you want to feel better about. This takes practice, as your mind will often default to thinking back to the negative thoughts as these neural networks are stronger than the positive ones.

As you begin to give more attention to positive thinking, these networks will grow and become stronger while the negative thought networks will begin to weaken. Over time, continually giving more attention to positive thoughts will cause the negative networks to fade away. If the network is not being used, there is no need for it and it becomes lost. This is the ultimate goal of cognitive behavioral therapy — to recognize the networks you are currently giving attention to and to refocus that attention to strengthen the more positive networks.

How does CBT work?

Cognitive behavioral therapy works by transforming your thinking patterns in the hopes of improving your mood and your overall life. While CBT is based on theory, its real-life applications have indicated a high rate of success. This is why CBT is a very popular therapeutic approach taken by many counselors and psychologists with patients. The theory behind CBT is that your thoughts greatly influence your emotions. What you think has a dramatic impact on your feelings. Even a single thought can create a violent burst of emotion within you. Now since humans are believed to think at least seventy thousand thoughts a day, that means that you feel at least seventy thousand bursts of emotion throughout the course of your day.

Negative thoughts are believed to lead to negative emotions, such as sadness and anger. If you frequently think negative thoughts, you are feeling nearly constant bursts of negative emotion throughout the day. If you feel more negative emotion than positive emotion, then your mood is obviously going to be lower overall. CBT believes that repeatedly subjecting yourself to bad feelings from negative thoughts lead to your emotional suffering. When you exist in a state of constant emotional suffering, your life can become rife with problems. You can also develop mental illnesses such as depression, anger, and anxiety because your constant low mood influences the chemicals in your brain. Life is much harder for people with mental illness because mental illness leads to poor judgment and physical symptoms such as lack of energy.

You may not be able to live a fulfilling life if your low mood and negative thoughts are constantly zapping your will to live and your ability to function. You don't have to suffer from your thoughts, however. It may not feel like it, but your thinking is totally at your disposal. You have control over your thoughts. If they seem to run wild, this is simply because you have not developed the strength you need to control your thoughts. This is how CBT can really help you. This therapy approach trains you how to take control of your thoughts. With this control, you can make your thoughts more positive and reject the negative thoughts that bring you down.

You can begin to heal your emotional wounds and recover from your mental problems if you are more positive. Imagine how good you might feel if you experience seventy thousand bursts of positive emotion rather than negative emotion throughout the day. Imagine how great life will be.

CBT is goal-oriented. It guides you to make firm resolutions to change your life. You are encouraged to find problems in your life and then find solutions rather than sitting around feeling miserable. CBT thus gives you the power to change your mind and solve your problems just by adjusting your thinking. Instead of thinking about how awful you feel about a break-up or problems at work, you can learn to think instead of how to make your relationship or work better. Overcoming and removing problems from your life will also make your thinking more positive because you have fewer stressful burdens weighing on your mind.

Randomized empirical studies have proved that CBT works. Various studies have been conducted on patients receiving CBT and patients not receiving CBT to see the difference that the patients experienced with their mental health. The results were then combined and analyzed to yield the conclusion that in simple English says: CBT really works. Patients who received CBT had faster results in recovering from their mental illnesses than patients who did not. CBT is actually able to change people's thinking and treat their mental disorders.

Five years ago, a psychoanalyst named Dr. David M Allen attacked CBT as a "simplistic approach that only treats simple problems." Sadly, Dr. Allen underestimated CBT. Studies have proved that CBT works, even if it is simplistic. Perhaps a simplistic approach is the best approach to the complex issue of mental illness. CBT also deals with very serious issues. The emotional havoc that thoughts wreak on you have serious consequences, such as mental illness, and CBT addresses these problems. Dismissing CBT as a silly new fad is missing out on a great method of healing.

After reading all of this theory behind CBT, you may be skeptical. CBT sounds so amazing that it must be very hard work. How can you possibly do all that by yourself?

Chapter 2: Basics of CBT

The history of CBT

Behavioral therapy (in general) has been around since the beginning of the 1900s. Some of the more well-known pioneers of varying forms of behavioral therapy are Skinner, Watson, and Pavlov.

Psychiatrists who study behaviorism believe in the idea that an individual's behaviors are able to be predicted, measured, trained, and (with some work with a program such as cognitive behavioral therapy) even changed. Behavioral therapy studies may have gotten their start in the early 1900s, but they have evolved and developed many new techniques since then. Different forms of behavioral therapy originally became a more popular idea after WWII in the 1940s, as many war veterans had to cope with harsh emotional adjustments when returning home from duty. The field of therapy suddenly saw a rapidly increased need for a form of short-term therapy that would be able to effectively help people cope with common mental health conditions resulting from the effects of war such as post-traumatic stress disorder, anxiety, and depression.

Suddenly behavioral therapies were used to treat a much greater variety of conditions than just emotional disorders caused by combat. These same therapeutic aspects and techniques were able to be carried over into other types of therapy as well as to be used in treating a large multitude of disorders, conditions, and mental health problems. The specific development of cognitive therapies themselves began in the early 1900s with a psychotherapist from Austria named Alfred Adler. Though Adler had originally developed the foundation of the idea for cognitive therapies, a lot of the further development of the therapies was performed by another psychologist.

The work of Adler was studied by and inspired an American psychologist by the name of Albert Ellis, who developed the concept of rational emotive behavior therapy (REBT). Rational emotive behavior therapy was first introduced in the 1950s and has since been considered to be one of the earliest known forms of cognitive psychotherapy. Rational emotive behavior therapy focuses almost exclusively on the idea that an individual's emotional problems and stresses often arise from their negative thoughts (resulting from a specific event rather than from that specific event itself).

The idea that an individual's condition may be caused by the thoughts generated after a specific event rather than from the event itself was a very controversial concept at first that eventually became the foundation for other therapeutic developments and studies. Albert Ellis was a huge advocate and promoter of the importance of behavioral therapies. The following quote is from Albert Ellis on the topic of his studies of various types of behavioral therapies and their results in treating multiple mood and emotional disorders:

Cognitive behavioral therapy is a concept that was first invented in the 1960s by a psychiatrist by the name of Aaron Beck. Aaron Beck was a psychiatrist at the University of Pennsylvania and was performing psychoanalysis on multiple patients of his when he noticed that most of his patients seemed to be having a sort of internal dialogue going on during their therapy sessions together.

An internal dialogue can be described as the personal conversation that a patient seems to have with themselves that often does not become audible or presented to other people, if a patient shares their internal dialogue with another it is often just a very small portion of what is going on in their head. An example of the internal dialogue a patient may have experienced during a therapy session is as follows:

"He's being quiet today." "Maybe your therapy isn't going well." "I'm trying my best to be open about my thoughts and feelings" "You've never been good at communication." From the above example of internal dialogue that may be present within a person's mind during therapy, they may only share the small portion of "I am often bad at communicating with others" with their therapist and may even begin to feel increasingly anxious as a result of these negative inner thoughts.

Psychiatrist Aaron Beck was one of the first to study and report the vital link present between an individual's thoughts and emotions. Beck has also become known for his thought that a patient's ability to identify their emotions was half the battle to resolving these negative and sometimes harmful emotions. During his psychiatric career, Beck designed and performed multiple experiments with his patients in order to test psychoanalytic concepts as they relate to depression.

Aaron Beck may have been a large influence on the growing popularity of cognitive therapies in the 1960s. As a result, there were multiple empirical studies performed on how an individual's cognitions directly affect their personal emotions, behaviors, and actions. This growing popularity and study of cognitive behaviors and therapies have become known to many as the cognitive revolution.

Since their introduction and further studies in the 1900s (especially in the 1950s and 1960s), behavioral therapies have been very successful in treating a wide range of neurotic disorders.

Despite their success in treating neurotic disorders, however, behavioral therapies have been unsuccessful at the goal of "curing" depression. Since its development in the 1960s, cognitive behavioral therapy has been the topic of multiple scientific studies as it applies to the treatment of a variety of psychological issues. Though developed in the 1960s, cognitive behavioral therapy had become increasingly widespread during the 1990s and still continues to grow in popularity today.

Modern cognitive behavioral therapy is a little different than it was when it was first developed in the 1960s. Today, methods of cognitive behavioral therapy are often combined with other types of cognitive and behavioral therapies. Some examples of other common types of therapies often blended with cognitive behavioral therapy in order to achieve greater success are multimodal therapy, pharmacological therapy, reality therapy, cognitive processing therapy, dialectical behavior therapy, integrative psychotherapy, and acceptance and commitment therapy.

Chapter 3: Your Thoughts

Negative Thoughts

Not all negative thoughts are the same. Work on properly identifying the type of thoughts you're having by categorizing them into some of the following distinctions:

Blaming

Becoming a passive victim of circumstance can make it extremely difficult to act on changing your situation. Blaming others for the problems in our lives can ruin relationships and take away our personal power. Not taking responsibility also makes you powerless to change. Blaming thoughts include "How was I supposed to know that", and "That wouldn't have happened if."

Always/Never

Thinking in absolutes and categorizing your views into extremes is typically made up of self-defeating thoughts. These types of thoughts typically include words such as "everyone" and "always" or "never" and "none." Black or white thinking can stem from a constant need for approval, being a perfectionist, and believing that attaining something makes up your value.

Take time to examine those irrational beliefs you may hold. Aim to create a balance between your actual and your ideal selves that is more realistic. These thoughts can include "They never listen to me", "I'm the only one that takes care of things", "I'll never get a raise."

Focusing on the Negative

An example of focusing on the negative would be if you had an evaluation at work. Your manager could give you 9/10 excellent marks - detailing everything that's great about the work you're doing and give a few notes on the one area that may need work.

When you're focusing on the negative, you're more likely to dwell on the one thing that needs work than the nine excellent things. When we allow negative thoughts to flourish, this can turn into a situation where you feel bad about yourself, resent your boss, and ultimately let it affect the work you're doing. Seek to find the positive and allow your thoughts to help you find more balance and optimism in situations.

Generalizing is just as bad. "That was a bad day." Was your entire day bad or are you only remembering the bad parts of it? This is a sign of depression that you'll want to watch out for. Look for the things you enjoyed during the day - challenge yourself to find a few things.

Thinking with your feelings

Our feelings are very complex and are usually deeply rooted in powerful memories. Feelings aren't always telling the truth either. When you have a strong negative feeling, examine it - is there evidence behind the feeling? Are there real reasons to feel this way? Typically, these types of thoughts start with "I feel" like - "I feel stupid" or "I feel like they hate me."

Fortune telling

Negatively predicting the outcome of a situation can really influence how you feel. We all have the chance to change, so even if you have behaved a certain way previously, it doesn't mean that you must do so moving forward.

Don't cut yourself off from changing because you don't think it's possible. For example, thinking "I never manage to make new friends at work events, I never have." Just because you never have doesn't mean that you never can. This type of thinking can lead to inaction - stopping yourself from having experiences and participating in life because you think you already know how things will go. Remember, if you could tell the future, you'd more than likely be a billionaire right now.

Guilt

Guilt is not a productive emotion and it can cause you to do things you don't want to do. Be careful to not use guilt to motivate or punish yourself and when making commitments and promises, don't overextend yourself. Guilt can be insidious and destructive.

Although separate from shame, guilt can eventually lead to shame when it's irrational or not absolved. These emotions have the opposite effect from increasing empathy and self-improvement. It's easy to beat yourself up and prolong these types of thoughts, and we tend to simply brush them under the rug by rationalizing our actions. These types of thoughts are repetitive and evoke progressively more intense feelings the longer we sit with them. Thoughts that include words like "have to, must, should" are typically associated with guilt. These negative guilty thoughts can manifest when we procrastinate as well.

We often don't want to do things simply because we think we must. A great way to combat those is by switching it from "I have to spend more time at home" to "I want to spend more time at home."

Mind reading/Projecting

These negative thoughts can manipulate your mind and are very common in those with social anxieties. Mind reading thoughts usually lead you to assume that other people are judging you negatively. Projecting takes your own thoughts and transfers them onto others - convincing us that they are thinking the same thing we are. We never really know what someone else is thinking unless they tell us.

Believing that you are a mind reader can damage the relationships we have with others, especially our significant others. It's easy to assume that you know what someone is thinking based on our past experiences, but we must be careful to clearly communicate with others. When making assumptions, we can find ourselves misreading someone's negative look to mean something personal when it could be something completely unrelated such as them thinking that their lunch isn't agreeing with them.

Labeling

We can become unable to deal with people reasonably and recognize them as unique individuals when we attach negative labels to them. This is also true when attaching negative labels to ourselves.

For example, if you think of someone as arrogant, you're likely to mentally sort that person into the same category as all the arrogant people that you've ever known. Be careful to challenge distinctions you are automatically assigning to people based on a situation, most times you'll find that someone's behavior in a certain situation isn't the only characteristic about them.

How would you feel if someone considered you the same way? Challenge any preconceived labels and work to discover a person's real character.

Personalizing

We can never fully realize why people do what they do. Personalizing the behavior of others and events with negative explanations can make us feel terrible and puts a distance between us and everything else.

These types of thoughts can lead us to become fixated on what's happening only to ourselves, and blind us from seeing the big picture. Assigning personal meaning to simple events such as a co-worker that didn't greet you can lead us to believe that they must be angry or don't like us anymore. Personalizing thoughts go hand in hand with catastrophizing thoughts - getting negative feedback on something doesn't mean you aren't able to become better or that it questions your worth. Our connection to experiences can be completely impersonal and doesn't necessarily need a response from you. Break free from this type of self-imposed solitary confinement by letting "what is", go about its business.

Exposing a lot of these thoughts to a more rational light can lead you to believe that you're just lying to yourself. Just because you've believed something for an extended period doesn't make it true. Most negative thinking is automatic and will go unnoticed. Use an intelligent perspective to review what's true and what's not. Write down these thoughts and respond to them. Take away the power they have on you and take control of your moods. Build that inner voice to keep these types of negative thought patterns in check. You can do this by catching a negative thought and identifying which type it is most like. Try to change the thought to something that is more realistic.

For example, "You never listen to me" would be identified as an "Always/Never" type of thought and we can change it around to "I get upset when you don't listen to me but I know you have listened to me in the past and you will again." Start to build positive thought patterns by approaching life more confidently and productively.

An easy exercise you can do when focusing on building positive thought patterns and associations is by using your 5 senses. Jot down a list of the happiest times you've experienced. Describe them in as much detail as you can. Where were you, what music was playing, what colors were around you, smells, people, setting, etc. Creating these paths of positive memory will strengthen your bonds. This will spur you to act lovingly and act on that feeling.

There are physiological and mental health issues that can seriously affect people above and beyond the bad moods and thought patterns most of us experience. Medical intervention can be required, typically antidepressants or herbal supplements such as St. John's Wort, but should always be discussed with a physician and your psychiatrist.

The Mind/Body Connection

Consider the mind-body connection. Our bodies, feelings, mind, and spirit are all interrelated and our mind-body wellness is in a reciprocal relationship with the way we manage stress.

If we don't feel good physically, the chances that we will feel good mentally are very low. Listen to your body and treat it with respect by giving it what it needs to function properly. There are easy steps to improve how you feel physically, and in turn mentally. Take note of your energy levels, what activities deplete you and what activities restore? Create a healthy balance by creating ways to nurture and care for all aspects of yourself.

Get out and exercise!

Endorphins make us feel good. Being active increases blood flow to our brain and the amount of oxygen available for our bodies to use. Physical exertion helps us to sleep better by normalizing melatonin and gives us a healthy appetite by increasing metabolism.

This doesn't mean you have to religiously perform an intense workout routine every day, it simply means that we should aim for at least 3 times a week for 20 minutes. Focus on some sort of aerobic exercises such as walking, weight lifting, or anything that keeps your heart rate up and the flow of oxygen to your muscles really going. Find what you like, make it an enjoyable event. Be sure to walk, cycle, or get some sort of physical activity every day.

Yoga can be extremely beneficial for people experiencing mental health issues as it combines breathing exercise, physical exertion, and stretching.

How to reclaim your thoughts

Once you feel comfortable challenging your negative thoughts, and maybe begin doing it automatically without needing to write it down, you can begin to replace them with positive thoughts. Simply challenging your cognitive distortions can help banish them. You may be noticing a decrease in the number and frequency that you have them. Changing them into something good is the next step to reframing your way of thinking.

Look back at your negative thought log. Do you see any patterns? It could be a reoccurring thought, or several thoughts about the same topic. Write this down in a new list. Next to each one, counteract it with a positive statement. It should be a much more positive version, but not straying too far from the original statement. If that happens, your brain is less likely to accept it as a fact.

When depression is at its worst, your brain tries to keep you from feeling better. It guards your positive feelings and protects them instead of letting you experience them. It's a way of preventing hurt and disappointment – if you aren't optimistic about something, you can't be let down if it doesn't happen. However, that's what keeps us in the cycle of depression. Our aim is to break that cycle so that you can begin to experience the good things again.

As an example, let's say a reoccurring theme in the negative thoughts is that you aren't attractive enough. Your opposing statement shouldn't be something extreme like "I am actually the most gorgeous creature on earth," because your depressed mind will immediately discard that as unrealistic. Instead, consider things such as "Beauty is subjective and different to everyone. There are people who find me attractive, and I have many qualities that I like about myself." This still gives your mind a bit of its protective habits to hang onto – you're not directly contradicting it, just introducing a new way of looking at the situation. Do this for any of your thought patterns, or ones that are particularly strong.

Start writing your opposing positive statements as part of your log every day. As you continue, you'll need to change them up a little bit so that they don't become simple rote things to be repeated. You can gradually increase the positivity. As you continue challenging your distortions and looking for the more optimistic views, you'll find that you can truly believe more of the positive statements. You can also choose positive statements that aren't directly related to the negative ones, but still dispute them. For example, if you think of yourself as clumsy, think of some times that you handled something well or with grace.

If you think of yourself as unintelligent, think of some times when you solved a problem no one else could or learned something easily. Your opposing statement would then be something along the lines of, "I can think of these specific times that this wasn't true, proving that it comes from faulty logic." If one of your distortions is to discount the positives or use a mental filter, you may find these exercises particularly challenging. It will take practice to identify the positives and learn to celebrate them. If someone says something positive about you, take it at face value. Don't look for ulterior motives or evidence of lying. Work on downplaying any negativity and focusing on the good.

For any situations that you find yourself trying to diminish or ignore the positives, write it down, and create a column for "negatives" and one for "positives." Write down anything that comes to mind for each, being completely honest with yourself. More often than not, you'll find that the positives are greater than the negatives, and you may find some you didn't notice without putting further thought into it. Find the positives in all of the situations you've written in your journal. Not only the ones that directly counter your distortions, but all of the positives you can find. A somewhat common example is when you see a disaster on the news, look for the people that are helping others.

Those people are a bright spot in the dark story and bring hope. Do the same thing with every situation you find yourself in. If you were scolded for something at work, but one of your colleagues cheers you up and says you'll do better next time. The positives of this situation could be that you learned a valuable lesson, your coworker's kindness made you happy, and your coworker confirmed some of your good qualities. One of the biggest components of our mood is how we talk to ourselves. With cognitive distortions in play, these are the statements such as "I'm not good enough" or "I can't do this." To start healing, you need to change your self-talk.

Evaluate your self-talk, and consider if you would say such things to a close friend. Most likely, you wouldn't. Give yourself permission to be your own friend. Start morphing your self-talk into a positive attitude.If you find yourself thinking that you're going to fail a test, cheer yourself up just as you would a friend – remind yourself that you can study, you already know the material, and you will pass the test.

Keep in mind the double standard cognitive distortion. It often applies to how you talk to yourself.

Even when you aren't directly trying to shut down a negative thought, you should have some positive affirmations ready to go. In your journal, take some time to write down all the good qualities about yourself. You can be broad, such as writing that you are intelligent, or you can be more specific with scenarios and situations that you handled well in the past. Out of each one, come up with a simple statement you can tell yourself.

Writing these out will help you see everything that is good about you, and having those affirmations ready in your mind or on the journal page will let you pull from them when you need some more positivity. It's very easy when we are depressed to get down on ourselves, but we need to remember our good qualities to keep from getting pulled into that cycle.

Positive affirmations also mean "talking yourself up," or telling yourself how awesome you are. However, there's actually a way that this can backfire. If you are too outrageous with your statements, even though you're saying them, you won't actually believe them. It's important to focus on the progress you're making, rather than making yourself sound perfect. "I am completely happy and successful, and nothing will bring me down," sounds false. Your brain will choose to dismiss it, and it can even lead to more negativity.

Instead, focus on the work you're doing. "I am making progress every day and getting better. I have changed my self-talk for the better." This is more realistic, and acknowledges the effort you've put in so far. It's a win-win. Here are some questions to answer in your journal that will help you pick out some positive affirmations for yourself.

- What are all the things you like about yourself? List everything, big and small.

- What do you consider to be your strengths? What situations do you always handle well? How so?

- What good qualities do you think that others notice in you?

- What are some recent compliments that you've received? How did they make you feel?

- List everything that makes you happy, no matter how small.

- What do you get excited about?

- Do you give back to others? How so?

- What are the morals and values that you live by?

You can also use positive affirmations that declare what you're going to do and how you're going to feel. For example, "I will wake up tomorrow morning feeling rested and energized.

"Many people don't realize exactly how powerful words are. In health care settings, you might notice the doctors and nurses often use the word "discomfort" instead of "pain." This is because "discomfort" is milder, and asking a patient about their pain levels may actually make them experience more pain. Just by planting an idea in your head with particular wording, you're more likely to experience it. This is why avoiding negative self-talk is so important.

Even if you're saying them in a humorous self-deprecating way, you're still planting that seed. Practice using milder wording in your life. Use "dislike" instead of "hate," "bothered" instead of "angry," "upset" instead of "despaired," and so on. To help you learn to find the bright side of things, start practicing counteracting any negativity with positivity. Expand past negative thoughts about yourself or your life.

Whenever you find yourself in a situation where you find something or someone a bit distasteful, take a moment to pause and look for some good qualities. Choose five positive things that you could say, and keep them at the front of your mind.

Finding the humor in somewhat negative situations can be a great tool to thinking more positively. It will likely come easier to some people than others, but anyone can usually find something to laugh at. There may be something funny in the situation itself, or if you react negatively in the moment, you may find that funny later. In addition to looking for the humor in your own life, seek out things that make you laugh whenever possible.

Watch stand up comedy or find jokes online. Laughter is actually a physical force that can change how you feel. Even if you're having an overall bad day, laughing can put you in a much better mood. Practicing daily gratitude is another good way to begin noticing more of the positive. Many people choose to write this in their journals, so that the thoughts are more fully formed, and so that they have a running list of things they are grateful for.

At a certain time each day, write down 3 – 5 things in your life that you are grateful for. Choosing the morning will give you a bright start to your day, or choosing the evening will give you a nice way to wrap up your day and reflect on it. However, you should choose whatever works best for you and gives you the time and quiet to focus on what you're writing.

The items you're grateful for can be absolutely anything. They can be something large, like the love of your friends. They can be smaller as well, like the ice cream you had after lunch today. They can focus on your thoughts and emotions, or more physical things. If you're having a bad day, they might even be something such as "I'm grateful that tomorrow will be here soon and I can start over." Make sure that your gratitude entries are at least slightly different every day. If you are too repetitive, your mind will begin to dismiss the items. They will become something rote that you write down automatically without putting much thought into them.

You want to really focus on these items and how they make your life better. No matter how small or simple they are, they should have some effect on you that improves your day. Here are some questions to use as journaling prompts to find gratitude and positivity in your life.

- List 20 things that make you happy.

- Did you recently face a problem that you solved successfully? Describe the situation and your solution.

- List everything you did well today.

- Can you think of a positive difference that you've made in someone else's life?

- Who in your life has a positive influence on you, and why?

The key to lifetime positivity is to become an optimist. Typically, depression turns us into pessimists, always viewing the negatives and expecting bad outcomes. These two groups actually have different ways of explaining things in their lives. Pessimist notice negative events more than positive ones. They'll see outside, uncontrollable forces as the cause of positive things, and themselves as the cause of negative things.

Optimists, on the other hand, notice more of the positive scenarios and see the negative ones as one-off moments. They attribute good things to their skills and frame of mind.

Master Your Emotions with Cognitive Behavioral Therapy

Even when you feel you fully understand and comprehend the effect your emotions have in your life, there is still a component you may not be able to gain full control over. Negative thoughts can be terribly discouraging. These thoughts have often developed and have been strengthened through years of negative self-talk. When you have such a strong connection with the negative dialogue in your mind, even though you try desperately to eliminate it, you can feel as if you are just not meant to be happy.

These thoughts are what can greatly hinder your ability to fully control your emotions. In this book, you will gain a deeper understanding of how negative thoughts impact your emotions, how they are hardwired in your brain, and effective ways to reprogram these thought patterns so you can begin to live a life of happiness.

Overthinking

Overthinking occurs when you try to take control and predict the outcome of a situation when you have little control over it. While it is important to be able to problem-solve and come up with solutions to things that cause you to have negative emotional responses, there is a point where this can also be taken to the extreme.

Overthinking isn't just trying to come up with solutions, it is constantly trying to avoid mistakes and risks you think you may encounter. You focus so much time and energy improving on possible solutions and finding every little thing that could go wrong that you never take action.

Overthinking can cause you to feel stuck, because you become overwhelmed by all the possible what ifs that you are unable to commit to finding a solution. This can cause self-doubt and will almost always cause you to miss the more joyful moments.

Each of these negative thinking patterns can be challenging to spot, since they all stem from productive ways to change negative emotions and thoughts. It is when problem-solving, self-reflection and seeing another perspective is taken to the extreme and no action is taken, then these methods cause more damage.

Negative thoughts are just like negative emotions. While they can cause us to have more negative feelings, when you look at them differently and understand what causes the root of the pattern, you can begin to learn from them. You can begin to better understand your negative thoughts by:

1. Observing your emotions. Since your emotions are the result of your thoughts, you can begin to understand what you are thinking when you pay attention to emotions. There are always certain situations, triggers, or people that can

cause you to think more negatively or more positively. Begin to recognize when each emotion arises — both the negative and the positive — and take note of your thoughts before, during, and after the experience. Through this process, you will likely notice patterns which cause you to experience more negative emotion due to negative thoughts.

2. As you begin to take note of your thoughts and the emotions that come with these thoughts, ask yourself why? Why are you experiencing that specific emotion? This will shine a light on the thought process behind them. Why do you think this way? Why do you feel this way about yourself? Most often, these thoughts will be assumptions that are not based on facts or truth, and often have nothing that supports the thought process. Keep track of these answers in a journal, so you can dig deeper into the true reason behind each.

3. By asking yourself why, you will begin to uncover where these negative thoughts are coming from. There can be a number of possible reasons for you to think negatively in any given situation — even

the most normal encounters can cause you to spiral into a negative thought pattern for what may seem like no reason at all. As you dig deeper and ask yourself why, you will see many reasons for what causes you to think negatively. When you have a list of possible reasons or assumptions, you can begin to uncover the truth behind each. When you have a negative thought, your brain works to supply evidence to support the thought pattern, even if the evidence is not fully true. After reviewing your list, you can look at it with a clear and open perspective to see what truth lies in each of the possibilities.

4.   In order to change your thoughts to more positive ones, you need to reword and redefine a new way of thinking. Once you have done this, you will need to take action to make these new thoughts true. When you complete this final step, you rewire your brain to come up with new supporting evidence for your new positive thought process, and this begins to help you think in a more positive way.

Changing your thought pattern involves looking closely at what causes you to default to the negative patterns, and then resolving the issues so you can avoid these negative thoughts in the future. For many, this is not something they can easily do on their own.

While mindfulness, gratitude, a healthy lifestyle, and stress-relieving activities can help you think more positively, they often cannot help you fully resolve where the negative thoughts are coming from. For many, therapy is a useful and effective way to really understand and change your negative thought patterns.

How does cognitive behavioral therapy work to help reprogram the brain

Cognitive behavioral therapy is an effective way for individuals to specifically identify the negative thought patterns they have. It then teaches them effective strategies to challenge these negative thoughts and change their perspective to a new positive way of thinking.

This therapy challenges the automatic thought patterns individuals have developed over the years. While it does highlight how past events and experiences can cause these negative patterns, the focus is kept mainly on the present moment and with the most recent situations. Cognitive behavioral therapy helps individuals clearly identify what their thoughts are, find the triggers that result in negative thoughts, and works to rewire the connections in the brain to focus on more positive thoughts.

This is why many of the techniques sound corny or full of fluff. The techniques used through this type of therapy require practicing gratitude, positive thinking, manifestation, and affirmations. All of these techniques work when one does them consistently.

This consistency is how the networks in the brain begin to strengthen — repeating a positive affirmation every once in a while will do little to strengthen your positive self-image neural networks if most of the time you are thinking negatively about yourself. While much of the techniques sound easy enough to perform, being dedicated and consistent can be more difficult. Participating in this type of therapy will provide you with the step-by-step process that will allow you to recognize your negative thought patterns, teach you how to specifically change these negative patterns to more positive ones, and to strengthen the positive inner dialogue.

When you are able to successfully accomplish this process, you will find it easier to overcome difficult situations and maintain a more positive outlook on life despite the struggles or challenges you may be facing.

What skills does behavioral therapy help develop in order to allow you to get out of difficult conditions? Through cognitive behavioral therapy individuals learn many ways to process emotions in a more healthy and proactive way. Cognitive behavioral therapy helps individuals become clearer when they identify a problem, and then allows them to set realistic and attainable goals for solving these problems.

Identifying the problem is the key to understanding what is triggering the unhealthy emotional response. Since many emotional responses occur because of our own perception and beliefs of a situation, cognitive behavioral therapies encourage patients to view things from a different perspective. This allows individuals to challenge assumptions, see the facts of the situation, and avoid jumping to the worst possible outcome.

Cognitive behavioral therapy helps you develop the tools needed to reframe your view of the world. Most often, our interpretations of the world are skewed and come from a place of negative emotions to begin with. This results in addressing issues in a way that does not help resolve problems or enable you to move on from what is keeping you emotionally stuck. How behavioral therapy helps you control your mental health by overcoming anxiety, anger, and fear

Negative thinking can lead to a number of mental health issues, from depression and anxiety to drug or substance abuse. These conditions are often the result of continuously allowing negative thoughts to take over your brain. Just one negative thought can open the doors, and usually invites more negative thoughts in. These pile up, one on top of the other, until eventually, you are living with a pessimistic view on life and are trapped by your own untrue negative views of yourself.

By taking control over your negative thoughts, you take control over your mental health. Cognitive behavioral therapy is just one of the many tools that can effectively help you transform your thought process. Cognitive therapy guides you through the process of fully understanding how your thoughts impact your emotions and behavior. A therapist helps you evaluate your own internal dialogue and recognize where this dialogue is coming from inaccurate beliefs.

You are then given homework and recommended to track your progress from one session to the next. These homework assignments are designed to help the individual challenge their inaccurate beliefs as well as find ways to disprove them. Through the process, the individual's inaccurate beliefs begin to change and therefore the negative experience that once overwhelmed them shifts. Since anxiety, anger, fear, and other negative emotions are greatly fueled by negative thought patterns, changing these thought patterns can, in turn, change the way you experience these negative emotions.

Cognitive behavioral therapy helps you feel more empowered, confident, and in control of what happens in your life. You develop the necessary skills to confront negative emotions through the process of self-awareness and self-reflection, and change your negatives to positives. Deciding to participate in cognitive behavioral therapy can be difficult. Often, people feel a great deal of shame when they decide that therapy is necessary to help them sort of their emotional issues.

While this shame can cause you to ultimately not take part in therapy, consider the outcomes. If you let shame win, you once again allow your negative feelings to dictate your behavior, and you are also giving the opinions of others more priority than your own emotional and mental well-being. While it can be difficult to finally agree to therapy, and it may be something you try to keep others from finding out, the benefits can be life-changing. Therapy can finally help you see pieces that you have been missing. It can help you make connections to your thoughts, emotions, and behaviors you previously never noticed.

If you decide not to participate in therapy, you can almost always predict that your life will remain in the same state it is in now. But by agreeing to therapy, you are giving yourself a great chance at finally living a life that makes you happy.

Chapter 4: The Benefits of Treatment CTB

In this section, I will give you an overview of the various benefits of Cognitive Behavioral Therapy. Firstly, it is amazing that this one therapy can help in the treatment of so many different conditions. As you gain a better understanding of Cognitive Behavioral Therapy, you may be curious about what exactly it can be used for treating.

Unlike what some believe, Cognitive Behavioral Therapy can actually be used to treat quite a few different conditions. It is also used as additional therapy, alongside other treatments, for various diseases to help the client heal faster and improve their way of life.

The following are some of the common conditions that can be treated with the help of Cognitive Behavioral Therapy.

Amongst many other conditions are the following:

- Depression
- Dysthymia

- Eating disorders
- Substance abuse
- Anxiety disorders
- Sleep disorders
- Personality disorders
- Aggression issues
- Anger issues
- Chronic fatigue
- Psychotic disorders like schizophrenia
- Muscle pain
- Somatotropin disorders
- Criminal behavior

Research has shown that Cognitive Behavioral Therapy has been used in the treatment of these conditions successfully for a very long time. Cognitive Behavioral Therapy has shown higher response rates when compared with other therapies used for the treatment of these conditions.

This is why psychotherapists all around the world tend to recommend Cognitive Behavioral Therapy in particular to their patients. The following are some of the major benefits of Cognitive Behavioral Therapy:

Helps Reduce Symptoms of Depression and Anxiety

The best-known treatment for depression is Cognitive Behavioral Therapy. Numerous studies show how beneficial this particular therapy is in alleviating symptoms of depression, such as lack of motivation or a sense of hopelessness.

This treatment is short term, but it lowers the risk of relapses happening in the future. It helps relieve depression because it facilitates the changes in thought process for the person. Hence they stop thinking negatively and try being more positive. Cognitive Behavioral Therapy is also used along with anti-depression medication. Some therapists also recommend it for patients suffering from postpartum depression. These are the conditions that are most commonly treated with Cognitive Behavioral Therapy.

Depression has become a very common condition in the last decade. As the stigma on mental health is slowly being removed, more and more people are being diagnosed with this condition. The causes may vary, but the symptoms are mostly the same, and it has a very negative impact on the person suffering from it. Depression can be a result of some traumatic event or even arise out of the blue. Nonetheless, it is important to validate this condition and give the person the help they need.

The hectic lives we lead also cause a lot of people to have anxiety issues. Cognitive Behavioral Therapy is very effective in overcoming both these conditions and helping the client lead a happier life.

It Helps Treat Personality Disorders

Each person has their own unique personality that others identify them with. How you come across to others is reflective of your personality. Every person will have certain good characteristics, along with a few bad characteristics. When a person displays more of the bad, their personality appears non-appealing to those around them. This can cause them to face various social issues.

Cognitive Behavioral Therapy can help improve such negative traits and develop more of the positive traits that will benefit the person and make them well-liked amongst others. Cognitive Behavioral Therapy can be used to improve someone's general personality as well as for treating various personality disorders that are a much more serious concern.

Helps in the Treatment of Eating Disorders

According to research, eating disorders have some of the strongest indicators of Cognitive Behavioral Therapy. Today's society lays a lot of emphasis on appearance, and this causes people to be much more conscious of how they look and how much they eat. This is especially so for women all over the world. This is one factor that causes eating disorders. They may develop these disorders to lose weight or even as a reaction to stress and anxiety.

Most eating disorders will fall under two types. One type is when a person develops a tendency to eat much more than required. This can cause the person to become overweight and develop weight issues. The second type is where the person may do the opposite and eat too little. This can cause issues like anorexia or bulimia. It is to be noted that these conditions can also be fatal, in the long run, if they are not treated soon. The human body requires a healthy amount of food to sustain itself well, and too much or too little can cause various illnesses in the body.

There are also people who have body Dysmorphic disorder. This makes them see their body different from what it really is. Even when they are thin, they might look at their reflection and criticize themselves for being fat. You have to understand that these kinds of eating disorders are quite strongly related to mental health issues. Your brain plays an important role in the development or prevention of such issues.

When there is an imbalance in certain hormones in your body, either type of eating disorder may develop.

It is important to identify the cause of any eating disorder and help the person overcome it. This is where Cognitive Behavioral Therapy comes in by finding the cause of any problem and then implementing techniques that help them overcome the issue.

Cognitive Behavioral Therapy has been extremely effective in helping people with eating disorders. It has helped identify the underlying cause of such issues and questions about why shape and weight are over evaluated. Cognitive Behavioral Therapy will help a person maintain a healthier body weight. They will learn to control the impulse for binge eating or the tendency to purge after eating. They will learn to feel less isolated and will also learn to be more comfortable around food that might normally trigger their unhealthy behavior.

Exposure therapy teaches them to avoid overeating even when their favorite food is right in front of them. Cognitive Behavioral Therapy is especially useful in helping patients suffering from bulimia nervosa. It also helps in treating conditions that are not specified either. Anorexia is one of the hardest eating disorders to cure, but research shows that Cognitive Behavioral Therapy is quite helpful in dealing with this condition.

Helps Control Substance Abuse and Addictive Behavior

At this point, no one is unfamiliar with substance abuse. Drugs are obtained too easily, and people tend to abuse their privilege as and when they can. No matter where you look, you will see that marijuana, meth, cocaine, and other such drugs can be obtained quite easily with a little bit of money. Going to the clubs or even walking down some streets will bring you across dealers who will coax you into trying these harmful substances.

A lot of people think that it's okay to try it once, but it is a well-known fact that once is just the start of a habit. Most people fail to exercise control over the consumption of such substances and deaths from overdose have taken an alarmingly high number over the years. Taking such drugs can cause a person's life to take a very drastic change for the worse.

It changes them, affects their body, and has nothing but a negative impact on their entire life. But for those who seek help on time, there is a way to turn things around. Cognitive Behavioral Therapy is one of the well-known therapies used to help addicts get over their addiction. The exact approach can be different for each person, but Cognitive Behavioral Therapy can help most addicts in getting over such harmful addictions. They will learn to control their thoughts, resist urges and take actions that will only benefit their well-being. And although it will take time, Cognitive Behavioral Therapy will train them in a way that they learn how to say no to drugs.

There is a lot of research that indicates Cognitive Behavioral Therapy is effective in helping people who are addicted to cannabis, opioids, alcohol, smoking, and even gambling. The skills taught during Cognitive Behavioral Therapy will help these people control impulses and prevent a relapse after the treatment is over. The behavioral approach is more effective than any control treatment.

Helps Reduce Mood Swings

Have you ever felt really low or really high? The answer will be yes for most people. Everyone has mood swings, but for some, it is not in the normal manner that others experience them.

Your mood is your current state of mind and it will affect how you feel and what you do. Sometimes your mood may be good and you feel very happy. The next moment you may feel very low and feel quite unhappy. If you have mood swing issues, your emotional state may be quite unstable. The smallest provocation may cause you to get angry and react in a bad way. It is important for people to have better control over their emotions and to learn to process them well.

This way, they will know how to react appropriately in different situations. Cognitive Behavioral Therapy is one of the treatments that can help people deal with such mood swings and be more emotionally stable.

Helps in the Treatment of Psychosis

Are you familiar with this term? It is a state where your mind starts losing touch with reality. In this state, your mind is pushed into a different world that is filled with sounds or images that lull you into a momentary but deep mental slumber.

People with psychosis issues tend to have very little contact with other people. Their mind tricks them into thinking in a very different way that is not healthy for them. Psychosis is more serious than you may realize. It can push the person in a way that their normal way of life is completely changed and not for the better.

Cognitive Behavioral Therapy is used for helping people who face psychosis issues. It is used to identify the root cause behind this state of mind and then the therapy helps them to establish a routine that is more of a normal way of life. The client will slowly move back towards reality and out of their virtual world.

Helps Improve Self-Esteem and Increases Self-Confidence

There are a lot of people who suffer from low self-esteem or self-confidence. They may not suffer from any serious mental conditions but having low self-esteem can cause the person to have very negative and destructive thoughts.

These thoughts are replaced with positive affirmations with the help of Cognitive Behavioral Therapy. This therapy helps the person learn better ways of dealing with stressful situations and how to improve their relationships with others. Cognitive Behavioral Therapy also gives them the motivation to try new things. Cognitive Behavioral Therapy techniques will help the person improve their communication skills and develop better relationships.

Many other conditions can be treated with the help of Cognitive Behavioral Therapy as well. There are even people who suffer from more than one condition at the same time. You also have to know that this therapy may not be effective in completely treating someone at times, but it makes a huge positive difference, nonetheless. This is why it is always worth it to give Cognitive Behavioral Therapy a try.

Cognitive Behavioral Therapy is a much more practical solution than most other treatments and it has helped a lot of people over the years.

Chapter 5: CBT Therapy

Panic attacks and CBT therapy

Similarly, to other mental health issues, panic attacks are also brought on by a source of fear. They can occur in people of all ages, but they most often occur in the lives of younger people, who do not have as many life experiences as adults to understand how to deal with a situation, or to have a scale which they can use to determine the seriousness of a problem. This is why panic attacks are so common in young people.

When it comes to treating panic attacks with CBT, the situation is a little different than in other mental health problems. The reason why is because panic attacks render the body almost helpless in defending itself once the panic attack starts. This means that in order to use CBT, or any other treatment method for that matter, in order to help with panic attacks, the treatment of thoughts needs to start before the actual panic attack. This is not easy to do because panic attacks cannot be predicted. However, there is another way that you can deal with this problem.

The steps for dealing with panic attacks with CBT are the same as the ones that we've outlined before, except that this time, it is the moment when you choose to use these steps that is crucial.

You will need to pick a certain time of the day when you can follow these steps, and then repeat the process every day at the same time. For example, people are usually he most stressed in general, when they get ready to fall asleep and then their mind decides to wander and think of all the bad things that have happened in life and all the opportunities that a person may have missed. This is a very heavy mind to fall asleep to right before bed time, which is why it is also the perfect time to take a moment right before bed and follow the steps for CBT to analyze your thoughts. Go to bed as you normally would, except bring a notebook and a pen with you, make yourself comfortable, and start analyzing every negative thought that usually comes to your mind at this time.

Focus on each thought, break it down into its source and what will happen if you were to follow it, and then exchange that negative thought for a positive one. Do this for every thought until you pretty much run out of them. your mind will then not only be empty of these negative thoughts, but it will also be tired of its own analyzing and it will decide that the best thing to do is to indeed just fall asleep. This 'before bedtime' tactic is great for dealing with panic attack issues, because it allows you to deal with all of your fear before your body even has the chance to make a big deal out of them and turn them into a panic attack.

Think of this as your most powerful weapon! You literally have the power to predict your panic attacks, and now you also have a way of dealing with them before they happen.

Chapter 6: CBT Advantages and Methods

In the present society, health practitioners and psychiatrists are speedy to prescribe psychotropic drugs which often accompany dangerous negative side effects for any disorder that is due to idea patterns.

But if you were told that there was a superior, more secure way to take care of and cure strain and mind disorders through cognitive behavioral therapy, would you try it?

CBT is just a form of psychotherapy which highlights the importance of inherent thoughts in ascertaining how we act and feel. CBT is regarded as one of the absolute most prosperous forms of psychotherapy to emerge in decades; CBT has become the focus of countless scientific tests. CBT therapists discover, investigate, and transform their particular thought patterns, and reactions since they are what creates our senses and determines our behaviors. Using CBT therapy boosts patient's quality of life and also help them handle stress better compared to patients battling with tough situations independently.

What may surprise you about CBT as a core basic theory is that extreme scenarios, interactions with different people, and negative events are not usually accountable for our poor moods and problems. Instead, CBT therapists view precisely the opposite as being the cause. It's our reactions to events, the more things we tell ourselves in regards to these occasions -- that can be within our control -- that wind up affecting our quality of life. This is great news because it indicates we can modify ourselves. Using cognitive behavioral therapy, we can learn to alter the way we feel, which in turn alters the way we see and cope with tough circumstances when they arise.

We are now better at intercepting disruptive notions that cause us to be stressed, isolated, and depressed, and likely too mentally obese and reluctant to change negative habits. When we could accurately and calmly start looking at situations without distorting reality or incorporating limitations or fears, we will be able to understand just how to react appropriately to help us feel better in the long run in a means that creates us feel speediest in the very long run.

Here are a few benefits of cognitive behavioral therapy:

1. **Lowers Symptoms of Depression**

    CBT is one of the most rapid, empirically supported treatments for depression.

Studies demonstrate that CBT helps patients overcome signs of depression: such rage and low drive. It also lowers their risk of relapses in the future. CBT is thought to get the job done well. It's known for relieving depression because it delivers changes in cognition (feelings) that fuels vicious cycles of unwanted feelings along with rumination.

An analysis published in the journal, Cognitive Behavioral Therapy for Mood Disorders found that CBT is protective towards severe episodes of depression and can be utilized alongside or in place of antidepressant drugs. CBT has also demonstrated promise as an approach for helping handle post-partum depression as well as an adjunct to drug treatment for bipolar patients.

Also, preventative cognitive therapy (a version of CBT) paired with anti-depressants were found to help patients that underwent long-term depression. Even the 2018 human study analyzed 289 members and afterward randomly assigned them to PCT and antidepressants, anti-depressants independently, or PCT with diminishing use of anti-depressants after healing. The study found that clinical therapy coupled together with antidepressant treatment was first-rate in comparison to alcoholism treatment alone.

2. **Reduces Anxiety**

There are strong indications that CBT could cure transmitted illnesses. Strong signs are seeing CBT cure for illnesses that are transmitted, such as panic disorders, obsessive-compulsive disorder, social anxiety disorder, generalized anxiety disorder, and post-traumatic stress disorder pressure disease. Overall, CBT shows both effectiveness in randomized controlled trials and efficacy in both naturalistic settings between patients with anxiety and therapists. Researchers have found that CBT functions well as an organic treatment for anxiety because it comprises various combinations of the following techniques:

Psycho-education regarding the character of fear and anxiety, self-monitoring of outward symptoms, bodily exercises, cognitive restructuring (by way of instance disconfirmation), the image along with in vivo experience of feared stimuli (exposure therapy), weaning from unsuccessful safety signals, along with relapse prevention.

3. Helps Deal with Eating Disorders

CBT has been proven to help significantly handle the underlying psychopathology of eating disorders and question the over-evaluation of shape and weight. Besides, it can interfere with the aid of sterile body weights, improve urge control, help prevent binge eating or purging, decrease feelings of isolation, and also support patients eventually become comfortable with "trigger food items" or situations using exposure therapy. Cognitive therapy is now the procedure of choice in treating bulimia nervosa and "eating disorders not otherwise defined" (EDNOS) the two most popular eating disease diagnoses. There's also evidence it could assist in healing around sixty percent of people with anorexia, which is considered to be one of the most challenging mental illnesses to cure or prevent from failing.

4. Reduce Addictive Behaviors and Substance Abuse

Studies have shown that CBT is excellent in supporting cannabis and other drug dependencies, such as alcohol and opioid addiction. It also helps people quit smoking tobacco and gambling. Studies published in the Oxford Journal of Medicine Public Health concerning solutions for smoking cessation have also found that working skills realized during CBT periods were tremendously helpful in cutting relapses in cigarette quitters and it appears to be superior to other curative approaches. There is also stronger support for CBT's behavioral procedures (assisting to stop impulses) at the treatment of problematic gaming addictions in comparison to control remedies.

5. Helps Improve Self-Esteem and Assurance

Even if you never suffer from any significant mental problems in any respect, CBT can assist you in replacing harmful, negative thoughts that cause low self-esteem, with positive affirmations and expectations. This helps open new tactics to handle stress, improve relationships, and increase the drive to try new issues.

6. Helps you become more rational

The brain essentially acts as a neutral object, giving a response based on the information at its disposal and also the way it was trained to respond. Cognitive therapy trains the brain to act rationally.

In CBT, it is believed that our thoughts lead to how we feel, behave and handle situations. The good thing about this is that we have a chance to change how we think and act right even if the situation remains unchanged. CBT helps patients to control the thinking pattern that leads to irrational behaviors. Those undergoing CBT treatment are thought strategies with which they can cope better whenever automatic negative thoughts (ANTs) arise. CBT helps to develop ways to control the brain.

7. It boosts your self-belief

CBT helps to boost your self-confidence and works on your belief system, so you gain much better control of your thoughts. With self-confidence, you will be able to face any challenge that comes your way to achieving success and attaining your goals.

8. It helps you stay calm and relaxed

The initial stage of learning about social anxiety therapy is to devise a new way to anxiety response. With CBT treatment one won't be frightened by anxiety or anything that happens abruptly as we approach things with much peace and calmness. It teaches one best way to handle different kinds of situations that may arise in a more relaxed manner.

9. CBT helps to raise your expectations as you expect better outcomes

Due to our prior history and self-doubts, we often expect negative things to happen to us. We are always expecting things to turn out bad for us. CBT works on those thoughts and your belief system so that you can start acting more rational.

As our thoughts and action become more rational, our expectations also turn out to be more logical as expert positive things to happen. With CBT, we are made to repeatedly question ourselves to ascertain if our old beliefs are rational or not. Are they fact-based? Alternatively, are they things that have been our norm for years, and we have never questioned it? What is the real truth?

Do we pay attention to feedback from others or do we only pay attention to our internal negative conclusions? Is there any chance that we've fallen into the trap of self-brainwashing over the years?

Our own old automatic negative thoughts can reprocess throughout the brain. Have you found a way to stop them? Have you explored the possible explanation for your actions and have you thought about it that there might be no justifiable reason to feel fearful and anxious?

As our belief system is transformed by our thoughts and beliefs which bring about physical changes in the brain. An improved way of thinking leads us to expect a different outcome, a positive one. Your outcome depends on what you think about the outcome.

Other benefits of cognitive behavioral therapy include:

- Preventing the relapse of an addiction
- Resolving issues in relationships
- Recognizing negative thoughts and emotions
- Chronic pain management
- Anger Management
- Ability to coping with grief and loss
- Dealing with sleep disorders

How Cognitive Behavior Therapy Works

CBT operates by pinpointing thoughts that continuously arise using them as signs for favorable activity and substituting them with healthy, and far more empowering alternatives. The heart of CBT is mastering self-coping techniques, offering individuals the ability to handle their reactions/responses of situations logically, alter the thoughts they tell themselves, and exercise "logical self-counseling."

While this helps the CBT therapist/counselor and affected person build confidence and possess a great romantic relationship, the power lies in the individual's control. How willing a patient is ready to explore her or his thoughts, be open-minded, complete research assignments and clinic patience throughout the CBT course of action, can all determine how favorable CBT will be for these.

Features that make CBT an Effective Tool

Pragmatic method

CBT techniques and theory are predicated on rational thinking, which means they aim to spot and use these details. Even the "inductive technique" of CBT encourages individuals to examine their own beliefs and perceptions to see whether they are realistic. With CBT, there is an inherent premise that many behavioral and psychological responses are all learned.

With CBT therapists' help, patients realize that their long-held premises and hypotheses are partially wrong, which reduces unnecessary anxiety and suffering. Feeling difficult or debilitating emotions: Most CBT therapists can help individuals learn to remain calm and clear-headed even if they are faced with unwanted scenarios. Learning to accept difficult feelings as "part of life" is crucial, and it can help prevent one from developing a bad habit. Usually, we become upset about our strong feelings and become more distressed.

Instead of adding self-blame, rage, despair, or disappointment to already-tough feelings, CBT instructs sufferers to calmly accept a problem without making it even worse.

Questioning and expressing

Cognitive behavioral therapists typically ask patients lots of questions to help them gain a fresh and realistic perspective about the problem and also assist them to control how they feel.

Definite Agendas and Techniques

CBT is usually done in a succession of sessions that all possess a particular objective, concept, or technique that work together.

Unlike a few other types of therapy, sessions are not exclusively for the therapist and individual to speak openly without an agenda on your mind. CBT therapists teach their customers the way to handle challenging thoughts and feelings by practicing particular techniques during sessions which may, later on, be implemented into life when they're most wanted.

Cognitive Behavioral Therapy vs. Other Types of Psychotherapy

CBT can be a sort of psychotherapy, which means that it calls for open discussion between patient and therapist. You may know about several other forms of psychotherapy and you're wondering what makes CBT stand out. Sometimes when there is an overlap between several types of psychotherapy, a therapist could use techniques from various psychotherapy approaches to assist patients in attaining their goals. For example, to help anyone with a phobia, CBT may be coupled together with exposure therapy.

How is CBT different From Other Popular Forms of Therapy?

The National Alliance on Mental Illness states how CBT Is Different from other popular forms of therapy:

CBT vs. Dialectical Behavior Therapy (DBT)

CBT and DBT and are most likely the most comparable curative approaches; nevertheless DBT depends heavily on validation or accepting uncomfortable thoughts, feelings, and behaviors. DBT therapists help individuals detect balance between acceptance and change from using applications like mindfulness guided meditation.

CBT vs. Exposure Therapy

Exposure therapy is a sort of cognitive behavioral therapy that's often utilized to treat eating disorders, phobias, and anti-inflammatory disease. It teaches individuals to practice calming strategies and little series of "exposures" to triggers (issues which are most dreaded) to become less concerned with the outcome.

CBT vs. Interpersonal Therapy

Social therapy concentrates on the relationships a patient has together with his or her family, friends, and co-workers. Focusing on societal interactions and recognizing negative patterns such as isolation, jealousy, blame, or aggression are part of therapy. CBT can be employed with social therapy to help reveal subjective beliefs and notions forcing negative behavior and supporting the others.

CBT Journal work

Journal work is the most important part of CBT; this might help you;

- Practice balanced and accurate self-talk.

- Learn how to change and control aberrations and thoughts.

- Use self-examinations to reflect and respond in healthy and better ways.

- Learn how you can properly comprehend and precisely assess emotional behaviors such as external situations and reactions.

- Through utilizing different methods it's possible to learn how you can live well and balanced with both your mind and body.

Once more, the duration of time a person spends in treatment is usually less compared to some other therapy. Also, note that CBT will not cure depression or other issues, but rather you will get measurable relief while improving your daily life.

Chapter 7: CBT For Treatment of Addiction

For over five years Dave watched his son Noel battle with methamphetamine addiction. By the age of 27, Noel had been to several different rehab and treatment programs, some of them helped in the short term but he would always end up relapsing and back on the streets and his parents were back to square one, terrified with nowhere to turn. At this point Dave had given up on the healthcare system helping his son. As a journalist he started to write a book about addiction and began to interview some of the world's leading experts about the nature of addiction and treatment.

Dave says that he was at his wits end, he was interviewing someone who knew more about the methamphetamine addiction than anyone else in the world but even he was unable to tell him where he could get the help that he needed. He asked other researchers and work colleges, but still no answer.

Since the experts didn't know, he decided to change his approach and began to interview people who had overcome addiction to find out how they did it. That was when he met Holly, addicted to methamphetamine for 15 years; she described herself as racked with demons she was unable to control. Holly went through the same ordeal, treatment center after treatment center yet nothing seemed to work. Until one day she was introduced to cognitive behavioral therapy, she was at the end of the line and believed she would die if she didn't quit. She has now been clean for 12 years.

Holly's success story inspired Dave to send Noel to one of the best cognitive behavioral therapists in the United States. Today Noel is 32 years old, five years clean, happily married and the author of two books about overcoming addiction. According to Dave his experience mirrors the medical field's lack of understanding concerning the problem of addiction and their ability to effectively treat it.

Today over 40 million Americans suffer from some type of addiction, whether its drug, alcohol or nicotine addiction. According to the National Center on Addiction and Substance abuse less than 10 percent receive treatment, and even less receive effective treatment. The last few decades have seen researchers develop effective behavioral and pharmaceutical treatments for addiction. However, in community and residential treatment programs such treatments are scarce and programs typically involve strategies such as "tough love" tactics which are rarely effective.

There are also the most popular treatment programs that the majority of people have heard of Narcotics Anonymous and Alcoholics anonymous which have helped many addicts at the same time as failing many others. There are many reasons for the treatment failures for addiction in America. These include a long history of viewing drug addiction as a moral failure as opposed to a disease. The health insurance industry has no interest in covering addiction, and a state wide problem of licensing standards that often do not require addiction counselors to have a great deal of training to effectively handle the problems that addicts deal with.

What Works

There are several forms of evidence-based behavioral treatments for substance abuse and cognitive behavioral therapy is one of the most strongly supported. Before you start working on the following techniques you will need to prepare yourself for change.

Here are the five key steps that you will need to follow:

1.   Write down the reasons why you want to change

2.   If you have attempted recovery previously why didn't it work?

3.   Set yourself measurable goals such as a start date to begin.

4.   Remove all reminders of your addiction from your workplace, home or anywhere else you visit frequently

5.   Let your friends and family know that you are committed to recovery and ask them for your support

Get a Support Network

Don't attempt to fight your addiction alone, it is essential that you have a solid support system and positive influences. The more people you have to turn to for guidance, a listening ear and encouragement the better.

Family and Friends: The support of family and friends is invaluable when it comes to recovery. If you don't feel comfortable turning to family because you have let them down in the past you might want to consider family therapy or relationship counseling to patch things up.

Build a Network of Sober Friends: Like typically attracts like so there is a high possibility that you have a lot of friends that are not sober. It is essential that you break free from this group of people because they will set you up for failure. It's important that you have sober friends that will walk you through your recovery. You might want to join a church, take a class, volunteer, or attend events in your community so that you can build your network.

Sober Living Home: You might want to consider moving into a sober living home if you don't have a drug free living environment or a stable home.

Go to Meetings: A recovery support group will provide you with the encouragement that you need to persevere with your recovery. It can be extremely therapeutic to spend time in the presence of people who understand what you are going through.

What Led to Your Addiction: Addiction doesn't just happen, there is always an underlying cause and it is essential that you find out what it is to ensure that it doesn't resurface. Did you start using to eliminate memories from a traumatic event? A breakdown of a relationship? If you don't deal with the root of the problem it will only resurface once you are sober. In order for the treatment to be successful you will first need to deal with the underlying causes.

Stress Relief: Many people turn to drugs or alcohol as a way of relieving stress, or to forget about painful events that have happened in life. There are much better ways that you can alleviate stress. You can learn to effectively manage your problems without reverting back to your addiction. Everyone is different; therefore, you will need to find the best techniques that work well for you. When you are confident about dealing with stress you will find that it is not as overwhelming and intimidating to handle it.

Exercise: Meditation and yoga are great ways to alleviate stress; you can also take a quick walk around the block.

Get some sun: Just being exposed to nature will quickly calm you down.

Play with an animal: Animals can soothe and relax you.

Smell: Breath in the scent of a flower, your favorite perfume or some fresh coffee beans.

Visualize: Take yourself out of the moment and visualize being in a beautiful scene.

Pamper yourself: Soak in a hot bath, or take a long shower, you can also give yourself a shoulder or a neck massage.

Triggers and Cravings: Getting sober is not the end of your recovery; your brain still needs time to rebuild the connections that were distorted while you were an addict. During the rebuilding process you will have some very intense drug cravings. You are going to have to make sure that you stay away from situations, people and places that trigger the temptation to use.

Coping Strategies: Cravings are going to come and they can't be avoided; therefore, it is essential that you already have coping strategies prepared:

Distracting activities: There are many things that you can do to distract yourself, these include: exercise, hike, a hobby, read, watch a movie or go and see a friend. Once your focus is on something else, you will find that the urges go away.

Talk it out: When your cravings occur, talk to sober friends or family members. Talking can help you to pinpoint the source of the craving and it can also help you to relieve the feeling.

Urge Surf: A lot of addicts try and cope with their cravings by just experiencing them. Some cravings are so strong that they are impossible to ignore. When this happens, it can be helpful to hold on to the urge until it passes. This technique is referred to as urge surfing, imagine that you are a surfer who is riding the wave of your craving, keeping on top of it until it breaks, crests, and loses its power.

Change and Challenge Your Thoughts: When addicts are experiencing a craving they have a tendency to remember how good the drug made them feel and forget about the negative consequences. You might find it helpful to remind yourself how bad the drug made you feel once you had come down off the high.

Chapter 8: Change Your Life for The Better with the CBT

To live a happy, fulfilling life, you will need to change your negative, unrealistic, irrational thoughts into a positive, more realistic, rational thought pattern. To start with, you need to admit and recognize that you have irrational-negative thoughts and rational-positive thoughts. Each one is formed a bit differently, and examples include:

• Irrational-negative thoughts

  - I'm definitely going to have a bad day since it is raining outside.

  - I should have never been born, then my parents would not argue and be on the verge of divorce.

  - I am going to be late for work and get fired because this guy just hit my bumper. I'm not going to be able to pay for a new one. I'm such a screw-up, and nothing ever goes right for me.

• Rational-positive thoughts

- The flowers are going to be blooming now that it is raining. They really needed the water.

- Although my parents are arguing a lot, their arguments are not because of me. I will show them love and support and help them resolve their differences without guilt.

- I am so grateful that no one is hurt in this accident. Although my bumper is damaged, it could have been worse.

Although therapy is part of the cognitive behavioral therapy process, we must remember that "therapy" here is not about the therapist doing the work for you.

It involves asking lots of questions. You must get comfortable with asking questions and then looking for the answers from within. Some of these questions can include:

- What are the reasons behind your thought that you will never be happy?

- What evidence do you have that supports this thought?

- Have you ever asked an individual you liked on a date?

- How often are you rejected when you put yourself out there?

- How often are you not rejected?

There are three types of problems that we face every day.

There is the practical: This is the situation which presents itself when you are trying to accomplish a goal, but there is an obstacle.

There is the emotional: This is the reaction to the situation.

There is the imagined: This is the situation that you invented in your mind.

For example:

The practical problem would be your car breaking down.

The emotional reaction would be that you get upset.

Although most people's reaction to their car breaking down would be getting upset, the actual car breaking down is not the cause of you being upset. Instead, you are upset due to your reaction to the situation.

In situations where you are experiencing emotional upsets, ask yourself, is the problem a matter of "want" or "need"?

Want is something you desire. Need is something that connects to basic survival. This includes air, food, water, or medication. Do you need the car to not break down? Does it threaten your basic survival? No, probably not. However, you want it to not break down because it makes your life easier and it's less expensive this way.

Reacting with a gut reaction is not going to help the situation, and it doesn't change the problem. It simply feeds into the negative thoughts that come up. It is an irrational reaction to a rational situation. So, by changing your thinking processes, you are able to live a happier life. When people suffer with irrational-negative thoughts, they spend the majority of their lives in an unconscious state of being. They do not realize these things are irrational and negative because they do not know anything else. They think that what they feel and think are just normal processes that everyone else also goes through. However, their thoughts and their mind are slowly killing them.

After they recognize that they are having these irrational-negative thoughts, they then have to admit to themselves exactly to what degree they are experiencing them. They also need to admit to themselves that their thoughts are irrational-negative thoughts, and think about how often they occur. Are these happening once or twice a day or more often than not? Admitting the truth to yourself is the most important step to being able to change them and deal with the thoughts.

With a bit of help from your therapist and by doing homework like the ones I will list below, you can help change your thoughts. These actions will change your life for the better, so following them is key to making changes.

First, each time you start feeling depressed or anxious, take out your journal and write down the thoughts that pass through your mind. Later, you will need to analyze all of these thoughts. Which ones are irrational-negative thoughts? How many of them are irrational-negative thoughts? Change these thoughts into rational-positive thoughts. Write down your rational-positive thoughts.

To make these changes, you will need to write them down every single day. This will help you eliminate those debilitating thoughts and change your irrational-negative thoughts to rational-positive thoughts automatically.

For a while, you will simply write those thoughts down on paper and change them into rational-positive thoughts. Eventually, over time, your ability to change them will become automatic, and this will be a shock when you do it the first time. That day that you stop yourself and automatically change the pattern of thoughts will be the one where you begin to change your life. Each time you do it, you will find that it gets easier and easier. Over time, it becomes second nature to you. At this point, you will have taken back the control of your life and mind. This will be an impactful moment in your life.

A few more advantages that come with the use of cognitive behavioral therapy when improving your life and living happier are listed below.

Greater presence: Cognitive behavioral therapy based on mindfulness can help you be more present for your friends and family. Mindfulness training has been known to increase the practitioner's ability to be more attentive to those that we care about.

By using cognitive behavioral therapy, the patient is able to translate the need to be present into an action plan that will make it happen. For instance, the next time you are discussing something with your partner, consider bringing your undivided full attention to the conversation.

Listen intently to everything they are saying. Practice listening as if this is the first time you have ever seen this person. Focus deeply on what they are saying.

Less anxiety: Living with anxiety can also take a toll on your partner due to the constant need for a support system they can provide. Oftentimes, those suffering with anxiety need a "safety companion," or someone that can help in times of panic disorder or agoraphobic episodes. For instance, when you have panic attacks, the other person has to rearrange their schedules to accommodate your needs.

This can place undue strain on the relationship. It can lead to resentment and irritability. With cognitive behavioral therapy, the relief of the anxiety will help the relationship improve since the anxiety is no longer controlling the schedule and damaging the relationship. Next time you are having uncontrollable anxiety, consider finding a therapist that is certified in cognitive behavioral therapy.

Improved mood: Depression can weigh on the family of the person who suffers it. It is hard for the one suffering to be enthusiastic about life or activities, they have low or no energy, and the sex drive, among other things, decreases drastically. With cognitive behavioral therapy over a 12- to 16-week time period, patients can start to feel better.

They will gain their ability to function without the decreased energy, their sex drive will improve, their enthusiasm for life will increase, and they will find more excitement in their activities. When the individual is suffering, the whole family suffers; when they are happy, the whole family is happy. So consider using cognitive behavioral therapy either on your own or with a trained therapist and see how well it can improve your life.

Better sleep: Twenty-three percent of adults in America suffer with bad sleep habits. When you do not get enough time to sleep, you will display irritability, impatience, and crankiness, and your personal interactions with family and friends can become shaky. Insomnia has been known to turn your bedtime into stress time.

This blocks the coziness of your bed and places you in an uncomfortable state for the whole night. It can even interfere with your partner's sleep patterns. Cognitive behavioral therapy can help with insomnia in 4 to 6 sessions. It can help a person regain the ability to fall asleep as well as sleep more soundly. It also helps restore the connection between their bed and rest and relaxation instead of stress. Consider cognitive behavioral therapy for your sleep-improvement needs.

Healthier relationship with alcohol: Drinking too much can be unhealthy for your health and your relationships. There is a higher divorce rate among those that over-use alcohol than any other concern.

It is also tied to the violence of partners and dissatisfaction among those in a relationship with an alcohol abuser. Cognitive behavioral therapy is a great way to target those thoughts and behaviors that fuels the alcohol problem, and it helps the sufferer find a better way of coping with their alcohol use.

Oftentimes, couples behavioral therapy is the most effective treatment. This is where both partners participate with the treatment plan. Since alcohol abuse is so severe, a life-long abstinence is necessary for continued success. There are treatment programs that will work towards a modest alcohol consumption, but in general, abstinence is best.

Happier kids: When children are suffering with phobias or anxiety, it can affect the whole family. Parents will suffer along with the child because they feel the strain from the child's refusal to participate in the activity they fear.

There is a saying that rings true in this case, "You are only as happy... as your least happy child." With each set of parents, there is a vast difference in parenting styles. One can be lenient, and one can be strict. Since the child is causing undue stress, the symptoms can amplify the parenting styles.

This leads to conflict within the home wherein parents bicker back and forth about the proper way to care for that child, leading to resentment and anger between the two parents. Cognitive behavioral therapy, along with behavioral treatments, has been found to be quite useful in these childhood disorders.

They can help all parties involved, not just the child. Consider trying cognitive behavioral therapy with your child, both in your own home and in a therapist's office.

Healthier patterns of thought: Cognitive behavioral therapy is not only used for mental health but for relationships and for communication as well. Since it is based on the connection between behaviors, thoughts, and feelings, to have reality-aligned thoughts means we will have a more positive behaviors and feelings.

The negative-irrational thoughts that enter our minds can be detrimental to our relationships. An example could be how your spouse continues to leave their clothes in the middle of the floor when they take them off. You, in turn, think, "he must think I'm his maid since he just throws his clothes in the floor. He doesn't care about me and all the things I have to do throughout the day.

He must think he works harder and doesn't have to clean up after himself. He doesn't value my work or my help in the home." These are all irrational-negative thoughts; there's no proof that they are valid. These types of thoughts interfere with the relationship and can end up driving a wedge between the two partners.

In cognitive behavioral therapy, the patient is supposed to notice the thoughts that we are continuously telling ourselves. They often happen so quickly and automatic that we do not even have time to connect the story in our mind to a real situation that took place.

Once you are able to identify those thoughts, you can begin to change them into rational-positive thoughts. Maybe your partner throwing his clothes to the floor has no bearing on how he thinks of your services— maybe he simply is too tired and complacent to pick them up.

His preoccupation could have nothing to do with your relationship status at all. Maybe your worries are more specific to a concern you are having from some other situation, and in that situation, it is a warranted feeling.

Cognitive behavioral therapy is not a treatment plan that advocates lying to the psyche. However, it is a treatment plan that helps us edit those negative thoughts into a more accurate positive thought.

Ask yourself these questions when you get upset with your spouse, friends, or family:

- What is the proof for the thought that I had?

- Is the proof contrary to my thoughts?

- Based on this proof, how accurate are my thoughts?

- How will I modify this thought to reflect a more realistic thought about the situation?

Intentions are enacted greater: We all want to be attentive to our partners. We want to be supportive, patient, and generous. As with any relationship, we have paved it with the best of intentions. However, if we are not deliberate with our values, then we risk leaving our intentions as mere platitudes that are vague and without any substance.

For instance, telling ourselves that family is the most important, then living completely opposite of that and placing them last. Cognitive behavioral therapy can be used even though you do not have a disorder to address. It is a great tool to use for sustaining action that is supported by our values. By taking inventory of your relationships and setting a clearly defined goal about them, you can begin to fix those relationships. For example, planning to turn your phone off during meal time and communicating with your family instead.

Collaborating with your family to help make this change is a great way to get everyone on board. A cognitive behavioral therapy program would include activities that are planned so that you stay on a specific path, such as placing action steps into a calendar. For instance, you can place "spend time with the kids doing something they love to do" into a calendar. The next step would be to protect that time slot from any other distractions. Consider having a conversation with your partner and seeing who they need you to be for the relationship to work. Then plan to move towards the goals set. Take note of any effects that happen within the relationship. The positive message about cognitive behavioral therapy: The most important message that you can take away from this book is that although many people will say that you cannot control your thoughts and actions, this is absolutely not true. You have complete control over your thoughts and actions. You were the one that created the thoughts, and that means you can change them. The basic understanding of cognitive behavioral therapy is that you have all the control in how you think and behave. When you are faced with situations that present negative thoughts, remember that you are the one placing those thoughts into your head. So simply tell yourself, "STOP!" and rewrite your thoughts to be more positive instead of negative. It can be quite hard to edit your thinking patterns. This is because you have conditioned yourself to believe these thoughts. So by being patient and by practicing the homework assigned by your therapist, you can begin to make true changes in your life and thought processes.

It may be uncomfortable at first, but it will get easier and easier. All it needs is practice. Imagine using your non-writing hand to write a letter or using your non-dominant hand to paint your nails. These things are uncomfortable to do at first, but over time, with lots of practice, you will eventually be able to do it with less discomfort. One day, it is going to be natural and automatic for you.

Another example of how this would work in a real-life setting can be connected to the practice of the law of attraction, which states that what you send out will come back to you. Thus, if you are sending out negative energy, then you will receive negative energy. Imagine that you are in a stressful situation and instead of using negative-irrational thoughts, you use positive-rational thoughts; see how the energy in the environment changes. You will, over time, start to draw in more positive thoughts and energy, and with this positive-energy shift within your life, you will be able to start living a much happier, healthier life.

Chapter 9: CBT Strategies for Overcome Your Fear, Panic, Anxiety, Depression, Anger and Worry

Cognitive Behavioral Strategies for You to Implement Today

Cognitive behavior follows a specific system that allows you to effectively implement this practice and experience full relief through your efforts. It starts by having you identify what the original thought processes are that are creating your unwanted emotional response and then moves into you finding a way to interrupt those thoughts so that you can eliminate unwanted behaviors.

When you are able to identify the primary reason as to why you are experiencing emotional responses to your environment, you can easily begin to change it and allow yourself to grow beyond your anxiety and depression. As you work through the following five steps, realize that you are going to need to apply them to every single trigger that you experience so that you can fully eliminate all of your emotional triggers. This can take some time, particularly if you have been struggling for a significant amount of time because there may be many triggers for you to work through. Furthermore, it will take several run-throughs of each trigger to retrain your brain to respond in a new way versus the way that it has been responding all along.

If you want to experience full relief from your anxiety and depression, however, you will need to maintain your faith and continue the process even when it seems like it is not working, as it can take some time for your brain to adjust. The more you run through your new reaction to your triggers, however, the more you are going to experience relief from your anxiety and depression. For that reason, it is important that you go through the new motions even if it does not feel like they are working because, even though you cannot feel immediate results, they are. Furthermore, in order to help you experience full relief, you should focus on working on your biggest triggers first and then moving on to manage smaller triggers later.

Attempting to override every trigger right off the bat can be overwhelming and may result in you struggling to maintain your changes. By focusing on your biggest things first, you can eliminate your overwhelming triggers and find yourself feeling significant relief rather quickly. You might find that, through this, some of your smaller triggers naturally dissolve because you are no longer living in such a high state of overwhelm and stress. Once these larger stresses are out of the way, if you find yourself dealing with any residual triggers, you can approach them in the very same way so that you can eliminate them as well. That way, you can experience more complete relief from your anxiety or depression.

Step 1: Locating the Root Problem

The first step in coping with anxiety or depression through CBT is to identify what the root problem is that is responsible for causing your anxious or depressive episodes. In CBT, this root problem refers to the environmental condition that is causing you to have a specific thought in relation to that condition, which subsequently leads to your emotional experiences.

The best way to begin identifying your root problem or problems is to sit down with a journal and write down everything that makes you feel either anxious or depressed. Be very clear on the specifics around these experiences so that you know exactly what it is that is stimulating your unwanted emotional response.

For example, if your family makes you anxious, be very clear on which family members are causing your anxiety and what it is that they are doing which results in you experiencing your anxious responses. This clarity is going to ensure that you can pinpoint the exact moment that anxiety begins in your everyday experiences with these individuals.

That ability to pinpoint the exact moment is going to give you the awareness you need to identify the moment in action so that you can apply your other CBT practices in order to help you overcome your responses. Make sure that you are exhaustive with this list, even if you are not planning on addressing every single circumstance right away. Developing an awareness around what is causing you to generate these feelings is an important part in being able to effectively mitigate your response to the environmental experience itself.

If you experience both anxiety and depression, make a list for each of these emotional responses so that you can start working on healing both of them. Once you have created your list of the things that make you anxious, you are going to need to review that list and determine what makes you the most anxious.

This way, you can create some goals for yourself based on what you desire to start working on right away and you can trust that the others will be addressed later on when you have more energy to do so. Make your goals with CBT very clear and descriptive so that you know exactly what it is that you are working towards. For example, if you deal with depression every time your spouse does not give you enough attention, your goal may be that instead of experiencing depression during these moments, you communicate with your spouse and work towards a resolution together.

Creating specific goals is going to ensure that you know exactly what behavior you want to avoid repeating, and what new behaviors you want to replace your old behaviors with. This is going to ensure that you can see just how far you are progressing and that you can make adjustments along the way if you find that you are not progressing as quickly as you would like to.

After you have created your goals, the next thing you need to do is to identify exactly what is going on in your mind when the root cause of your emotions is occurring. Ask yourself what thoughts you are having during those experiences and how those thoughts are contributing to the development of your anxiety.

For example, maybe when you experience anxiety from your boss wanting to talk to you, your immediate thoughts are "What have I done wrong? Why can I never do anything right? I'm going to get fired, I won't be able to afford rent or food, I'm going to be homeless and hungry! Why can't I do anything right?"

These thoughts are obviously going to trigger an anxious response because your immediate fear is that you are somehow going to be in danger of losing your living and the lifestyle that you have created for yourself. If you are unaware of the exact thoughts that you are experiencing, you might consider using a thought record which is a tool that is commonly used in CBT.

The thought record allows you to record your thoughts during your anxious experiences so that you can begin to identify exactly what it is that you are experiencing in your moments of anxiety. On your thought record, you need to include the time, the external trigger, the thought, the intensity of the thought, and the intensity of your emotional response.

Keeping a record of these can help you identify where your troubling experiences lie and what you need to adjust in your mind through the CBT process in order to eliminate your anxious responses. You might consider using the thought record throughout the entire process to help you track your improvements if you are finding it difficult to see your own growth within yourself.

Step 2: Writing Self-Statements

Self-statements refer to the thoughts that you are experiencing in your mind regarding yourself and how you view yourself in various circumstances in your life. Our self-statements are generally divided into two categories — positive and negative. Positive self-statements are how we reinforce ourselves from within and essentially praise ourselves for positive behavior or for something that we feel we did right.

For example, if you were praised by your boss for having done a great job on a recent project, your self-statements might be "Wow, I really am good at what I do! I'm a great person!"

Alternatively, negative self-statements are how we reprimand ourselves for doing something that we believe was done poorly or wrong. For example, if you were told by your boss that you need to do better because she was not impressed by your recent performance, you might instead think "Wow, I really do suck. Look at how badly I performed. I'm a bad person."

For people who are experiencing anxiety or depression, it can pretty well be guaranteed that they are also experiencing negative self-statements in their mind. Often times, when you are experiencing anxiety or depression, your self-statements are extremely negative and you may even repeat them over and over again in your mind as you essentially punish yourself for being "bad."

Studies have shown that negative self-statements are something that we use to attempt to persuade ourselves into behaving better, by believing that through placing a high pressure *against* doing something wrong, we can encourage ourselves to change. Unfortunately, this is not actually correct, as negative self-statements will not encourage you to change your behavior, but instead, may actually increase your negative behaviors or emotional responses by increasing your internal stress levels.

What you need to do instead is use positive self-statements that encourage you to look beyond your failures and begin seeing the areas in your life where you are doing positive things. In a sense, you want to use these statements to help yourself see "the silver lining" in your behaviors. Now that you already have a sense of what your biggest problem areas are and what your thoughts are around those problem areas, you can probably identify areas where you may be experiencing negative self-statements.

With clarity around what those statements are, you can begin to consciously and intentionally re-write those statements so as to eliminate the stress that you are experiencing in relation to your environmental conditions. Rewriting these statements are going to require for you to do two things: First, you need to intentionally rewrite the statement so that you have something positive to say to yourself when your trigger is being stimulated.

Second, you need to ensure that you are actually using those statements when your triggers are being stimulated so that you can begin experiencing the positive benefits of them. Some people call this "using affirmations" because your goal is to affirm your positive self-statements to yourself often enough that your negative self-statements begin to dissolve and you start genuinely believing the positive self-statements.

At first, you may struggle to believe these self-statements because you are so used to believing and attaching yourself to the negative self-statements that you have been feeding yourself. As you continue to affirm these new positive self-statements to yourself, however, you will find that you begin to actually believe them and feel better about yourself.

The best way to get started in writing positive self-statements is to sit with your thought log and identify how you can completely flip the script on your negative self-statements that you seem to cling to.

For example, maybe you are disabled and you find yourself regularly repeating negative self-statements around your disability because you feel as though it has taken away from your quality of life. Maybe your negative self-statements that arise every time you find something that is a challenge for you are something like "I am incapable, I will never be able to do anything good again. I am a loser, why can't I be normal like everyone else?"

These negative self-statements will obviously not improve your sense of wellbeing, but when you are in the emotional state, you may feel like there is no other option for how you can feel or what you can think. The reality is that this is not true and that the one thing that you are always in control over is how you choose to think and feel.

So, you can choose to change the script on your negative self-statements to reflect something that is more positive and affirming of yourself and the abilities that you do have. For example, maybe instead you would say "I am capable of doing so many other things, I accept that I cannot do this one thing. I am a wonderful person and I choose to be grateful for the life I have."

By choosing to be grateful for what you do have and what you can do rather than feeling defeated and depressed because of what you do not have or what you cannot do, you make the conscious choice to change your experience. Rather than experiencing so much self-defeat and self-pity, you enable yourself to choose to see and live within the good aspects of your life and use those to keep yourself feeling positive and hopeful. You need to do this with every single negative thought that you experience when you are facing the triggers that typically ignite your anxiety or depression. Ideally, you should have these new positive self-statements rewritten and kept nearby so that you can repeat them to yourself every time you begin experiencing the negative self-statements.

If you find yourself in a position where your trigger has been stimulated and you experience a new negative self-statement in your mind in response to that trigger, simply make the decision to change it by reversing it completely. Then repeat your new positive statement in your mind until you begin feeling better around the trigger that has been stimulated. Over time, the repetition will retrain your brain so that you can begin experiencing a complete change in your reality.

Step 3: Finding New Opportunities for Positive Thinking

In addition to re-writing your self-statements, you should also seek out new opportunities for positive thinking even when your trigger has not necessarily been pulled.

Finding new opportunities to think positively in situations that previously resulted in you feeling tremendously negative can retrain your brain to see things in a more positive light, including those things that previously brought you anxiety.

These new opportunities should be sought when you are feeling a peaceful or neutral state of mind so that you can begin adjusting your overall feelings towards your trigger in general. This way, you do not find yourself living in a constant state of discomfort, worry, or alertness as you attempt to remain prepared to respond to the things that bring you anxiety or depression in your life. For example, let's say that you experience anxiety because a certain co-worker of yours is a bully and has repeatedly treated you poorly over the years despite your best efforts to improve the situation and make work conditions better for yourself.

Perhaps you only experience a panic attack after the bullying has begun, but because of that, you find that you are feeling on edge every single time that co-worker is scheduled to work the same shift as you. You might even find yourself on edge every time someone else brings up that co-worker's name because you are so anxious about the negative experiences that you have had with this person in the past. As a result, your constant state of mind is going to be negative and anxious around this person, which will only further increase your anxious responses any time this person bullies you.

Not only will this increase your unwanted emotional responses, but it will also decrease your ability to actually stand up for yourself and assert your boundaries around this particular person. As a result, the unwanted experience will continue happening no matter what you do. By finding a new way to think positive around your anxious experiences and just in general, you empower your mind to move into a state of rest rather than existing in a chronic state of worry. This way, you are far more likely to manage your emotions in a more meaningful and effective manner that actually allows you to achieve the results you desire or need from the unwanted experience.

You can do this by intentionally creating time to monitor and adjust your thoughts around the trigger itself, even when you are not being actively triggered. As you are thinking about the thoughts around the upsetting experience, consider what your thoughts sound like and begin rewriting them. Just like you did with your self-statements, find a way to empower yourself by flipping the script and rewriting your thoughts in a new and more positive manner. For example, rather than thinking "I really hope I don't work with so and so today! I can't handle when they are around, they treat me so badly!" Instead, think "I'm so grateful that I have a great job that allows me to pay my bills.

If so and so is there today, I am going to assert myself and if it doesn't work, I am going to seek support from HR." By having a clear action plan in place and thinking empowering thoughts, you literally empower yourself to change your experience around your triggers.

Step 4: Implementing Daily Visualization Practices

Another powerful tool that is commonly used in CBT is visualization as it helps you to see yourself behaving differently from how you normally behave in your life.

With visualization, you can visualize your triggering experiences and then intentionally visualize yourself responding to those triggering experiences in a more positive and intentional manner. Visualizing yourself behaving differently has actually been proven to teach your brain how to respond differently in situations that previously resulted in you experiencing anxious or depressed triggers.

In one study done at the University of Chicago by Dr. Biasiotto, he discovered that by encouraging basketball players to visualize themselves practicing basketball, they could experience significant improvement in their skills. Dr. Biasiotto discovered through his study that players who actually practiced playing and those who only visualized their practice and never physically practiced were almost on par for their improvements in their performances.

If visualizing themselves practicing basketball without ever actively practicing their skills can help basketball players improve their abilities, imagine what it can do for you when it comes to enduring your own triggers? Clearly, visualization is a powerful aide and that is exactly why it is such a fundamental part of CBT.

Through visualization, you can begin training your brain to improve the way it responds to negative triggers, which can ultimately result in you eliminating those triggers altogether in the long run!

In order to begin using visualization in your own CBT practice, all you need to do is consider your biggest triggers and spend some time visualizing how you would respond differently if you felt that you had more control in those situations. For example, maybe you experience depression every time you realize that you are trying to build a business but you cannot seem to earn any income through your business. Perhaps you are feeling like a failure and like maybe, being an entrepreneur is not for you because you cannot seem to create any success in your venture and so you are feeling rather down on yourself.

In your visualization then, you would picture yourself handling your setbacks with greater intention and success so that you can begin earning money through your business. By visualizing yourself closing sales and easily attracting customers into your business, you can begin changing the way that you approach your business and the confidence that you have in yourself as a business owner.

As a result, you will likely see greater improvements in your company and greater motivation within yourself to create those improvements, rather than feelings of defeat and depression. You should engage in your visualization practice for at least 10 minutes every single day, as research has shown that 10 minutes is the amount of time that you need in order to change your entire experience.

Simply set a reminder or an appointment in your phone every single day for you to begin your visualization practice and then set your timer for 10 minutes. Then, close your eyes and visualize your successful ability to navigate challenging experiences for 10 minutes. The more you do this, the more confidence you are going to feel around this particular area of your life and the easier you are going to be able to navigate it successfully in real life.

Step 5: Accepting Disappointment and Pain

The last part of CBT is that you are going to need to learn is how you can accept disappointment and pain. Although you will learn more about this within ACT, it is a fundamental part of CBT as well, as this acceptance enables you to realize that you may not ever be able to fully eliminate the trigger that you are facing in your life.

Instead, you may simply need to be willing to accept that it is always going to be challenging for you to navigate and that you will always need to exert a consistent amount of effort in successfully navigating it. When you are able to accept that things may never be great, you can stop holding on to the belief that everything is going to change and suddenly be easier for you.

For example, if you can accept that your Mom is always going to be unkind towards you because you decided to drop out of college to travel the world, then her consistent jabs towards you for your decision will no longer hurt so much. They may still be annoying and they may still cause you to feel bad, but through acceptance and the implementation of other CBT practices, they will no longer cause for you to have such intense emotional responses towards them.

Creating acceptance around the things that you cannot control and acceptance around the feelings of disappointment and pain in and of themselves can create a significant amount of peace within you because you stop trying to run away. Rather than trying to escape the pain or the stress, you can simply recognize it for what it is and appreciate that it is always going to exist for you. However, because you are no longer trying to escape it, you stop creating unnecessary disappointment and pain in your own life by letting the suffering consume you.

As a result, you are able to minimize the impact of the trigger and experience significant relief around it altogether. This may not be an opportunity to completely eliminate your emotional responses to the things that you experience in your life, but it can certainly support you in taking back control over them. That way, even though you are still emotionally responding, you do not feel as though you are at the mercy of your emotional response.

Chapter 10: Putting CBT To Practice

This chapter majorly focuses on putting cognitive behavioral therapy into practice on specific problems, such as depression and anxiety. We will show you how to overcome the disorders and improve your relationships. An important initial step in dealing with a psychological problem is learning more about it, also known as psychoeducation. This form of learning gives you the relief of knowing that you are not alone and that other people have found useful methods of overcoming it.

You may also find it useful for your friends and family to learn more regarding your problem. Some individuals find that having a proper understanding of their worries is a huge positive step towards recovery. For instance, a person suffering from recurrent panic attacks should begin by understanding what they are. One is likely to discover that while a panic attack is an irritating experience, it is not dangerous and does not last. Psychoeducation is important, but it is significant to note that this is just one part of a whole treatment plan.

Taking an Axe to Anxiety

Anxiety is a feeling that brings many uncomfortable bodily sensations. Essentially, it is what one feels in response to an intimidating situation. One may undergo anxiety as an extreme fear in the case of phobias, devastating physical emotions in the case of a panic disorder, or a reasonably constant feeling of agitation and unease.

Anxiety can come in various forms and may affect anyone in society regardless of the status. Anxiety is no fun. It can be enormously uncomfortable and unpleasant. Severe anxiety can interfere with one's ability to live an enjoyable life. To the extreme, you may find that anxiety restricts your interaction with others, stops you from leaving your house, or prevents you from working as expected.

People can become anxious following distinguishable traumatic events. However, anxiety slowly builds without you being able to do anything about it. In this chapter, we will show you how to face and tackle anxiety and how to overcome it. No matter what form your anxiety has taken, the methods in this chapter are likely to help to you. You may have identified symptoms of an anxiety disorder or your psychiatrist or doctor may have diagnosed you with it.

It can be useful to have a clear verdict or diagnosis of your specific type of anxiety disorder; however, using this chapter will help you to deal with your anxiety whether you have been granted a formal diagnosis or not.

Philosophies That Fend Off Fear

To say the least, anxiety is uncomfortable. We don't want to invalidate your personal experiences, physical symptoms, or disturbing thoughts, but we would like to encourage you to put on some anti-fear attitudes.

Think of these nervous feelings as a bully who is trying to show you that he is tougher, bigger, and more dangerous than he really is. You need to bring this kind of intimidation to an end! Anxiety involves the below ways of thinking:

- Overemphasizing the chance of a negative event/threat occurring.

- Overemphasizing how bad it will be if the negative event/threat did occur.

- Underrating your ability to surmount or cope with the negative event/threat.

Overcome your anxiety and fears by using below ways of thinking as your weaponry:

- Be realistic on the chances of the negative event/threat occurring: "It might happen, but it is not as probable as I imagine."

- Bring the badness of the negative event/threat into perspective. This tactic is known as anti-awfulizing: "It is bad but not awful, unfortunate but not terrible, tough but not horrid, and hard but not tragic."

- Give yourself credit for your coping abilities so far. Hold a high endurance philosophy: "It is not comfortable, but I can tolerate it," "It is hard to endure, but I can do it," or "It is difficult to bear, but it is still bearable."

The subsequent sections will give you chances to put these worry-defusing philosophies into practice with your specific symptoms and anxiety problems.

Surfing Bodily Sensations

Anxiety and depression come with so many mental and physical sensations. The sensations can be frightening and intense. If you have experienced panic attacks, you are possibly not a stranger to the numerous symptoms.

It is all too easy for you to mistake your physical feelings as serious or dangerous signs of bad health. If you do not recognize your mental and physical sensations as part of anxiety, you are likely to mistakenly think that you are going crazy, having a heart attack, unable to breathe, going to pass out, or even die. It is fathomable that one will want to halt their symptoms and try to control them. These efforts to fight against the bodily sensations of anxiety nearly always have an absurd effect.

One freaks out about their anxious sensations, and by trying to control or eradicate them, he/she worsens and perpetuates them. The attempts to stop, avoid, or reduce physical feelings are also safety behaviors. See your psychiatrist if you have a real health problem that requires medical attention. It is always important for you to get a clean bill of health before getting yourself into the exposure exercises, which may assist you with your irritating physical symptoms of anxiety.

Being Realistic on the Likelihood of Bad Events

When individuals suffer from any anxiety problem, they fear bad things will happen and are inclined to assume they are very probable to occur.

Whether one worries about becoming sick, harm coming to them or loved ones, having a panic attack, or being socially rejected, he/she overestimates the probability of the bad things occurring. Anxiety can affect how you reason and think to a notable degree.

Bringing Bad Activities Back into Perspective

Anxiety often leads one to make a dreaded event more awful in their mind than it is in actual life. When anxiety strikes, one tends to blow negative/bad events out of proportion and often decide they are unbearable, awful, and world ending. Fortunately, events are rarely this terrible. Usually, one would cope with their feared event no matter how difficult or uncomfortable it may be.

Ways of thinking that are anti-anxiety in nature involve increasing beliefs in our ability to handle unpleasant events and sensations. Always tell yourself that you can and that you will cope with the anxiety – although it is not an easy thing to do. Remember that you have been through episodes of panic and fear before, and despite finding it uncomfortable, you have survived. You can also try developing improved attitudes on the likelihood of other individuals negatively judging you. Do not attach too much importance on what other people may think of you as it might lead you to feel even more worried and anxious. Instead, remind yourself and always have an attitude like, "It is unfortunate if people think negatively about me, but it is not unbearable or terrible."

Keep in mind that no matter how embarrassing your symptoms of anxiety may be; others may be more understanding and compassionate than you would expect.

Exposing Yourself

At this point one needs to do exposure exercises. They involve identifying your worries and fears and planning to face them. Facing one's fears in a deliberate and planned manner is the best way one knows to overcome an anxiety disorder.

Although facing fear is not fun, it is efficient. Think about how unhappy you are because of your anxiety disorder. Have you really had enough of living life through a veil of fear? Would you consider going through temporary pain doing exposure exercises if it is worth it for a lasting gain of overcoming anxiety? The following list is important for implementing effective exposures:

- Make the exposures adequately challenging to be uncomfortable but not so devastating that you would unlikely stick to the technique.

- Continue exposing yourself to dreaded situations/events frequently, and each time make them gradually more challenging. One time isn't enough. As a rule, keep exposing yourself to these fears until you become desensitized or habituated to them.

- For the exposure sessions to work, ensure that they are long enough. Remain in the situation/event until your anxious sensations reduce by approximately 50 percent.

- Try avoiding or controlling aspects of your anxiety by taking note of the things you do. During the exposure sessions try as much as possible to resist any safety behaviors/actions.

- Remind yourself of the acronym FEAR in CBT. It means Face Everything And Recover.

- Believe that you can tolerate, accept, and cope up with discomfort brought about by anxiety. You do not have to love it, but you can endure it.

- Record how your exposure works and keep your notes so that you can trend and track your development and progress.

Preparing Your Exposure Plan

Now you will need to transform your intention into action. Many people delay starting exposures unless they create time for it. Honestly, exposing oneself to fears is not a walk in the park, so quitting is easier than maintaining it. Quitting exposure sessions in the present can also mean putting up with fear and anxiety in the future. Often exposures are not as bad as one may think it is.

The more often one does exposure exercises, the faster they can overcome their anxiety disorder. For instance, one may record things, such as answering phone calls, going to the supermarket, and sitting in her garden, as her first three exposure activities. These become the first goals of specific exposure events to confront. Now figure out the day and the time you will do your preliminary exposure session. Commit yourself to a particular time to do it. Assign times to redo the same exposure session as repetition is key to overcoming anxieties. Do not leave a gap of more than a day between two repetitions if possible.

The more often the exposure sessions the better. The time one should spend in an exposure work is likely to vary, but the rule of thumb remains in the situation until the anxiety has meaningfully diminished by about 50 percent.

Ways Out of Wearisome Worry

When one has any anxiety disorder, the probability that one becomes worried is high. Most individuals get worried from time to time. To avoid worrying all together, you would not care about anything. Nonetheless, there is a huge difference between unhealthy anxiety and healthy concern. The initial involves unproductive fear and worry. Worry takes up a lot of our time and energy, is unproductive, and triggers anxiety.

If you realize that your present most persistent worries do recur repeatedly even though in somewhat different forms and means, then you have some worry themes that are definite. This can mean you worry about these spheres of your life excessively even when there nothing wrong. The most common worry themes include relationships, finances, health, and others' opinions about you.

If you have been anxious a long time, chances are you may not comprehend that you can train your mind to be free from worrying thoughts and feelings.

Worrying is a dangerous habit, and with perseverance and tenacity you can overcome it. Breaking it means a lot of sacrifice and hard work, but the outcome is worth it. One tends to feel vulnerable and strange when they start resisting their worry habit. But in a matter of time, you will get accustomed to the sweet reprieve of not being a constant worrier anymore. Do not give yourself much time to worry. Engross yourself in events and activities to redirect your attention from worrying thoughts.

Pick activities that need concentration like doing accounts, listening to others, or solving puzzles. In so many ways, exercise can be of great value to you and can aid in "sweating out" your worries.

Relaxation Strategies

Learning how to relax one's body can be a useful part of therapy. Shallow breathing and muscle tension are both linked to anxiety and stress. So, it is vital to be aware of the bodily sensations and to frequently practice some exercises to learn how to relax. The two strategies that are usually used in CBT are progressive muscle and calm breathing. Calm breathing involves deliberately slowing down one's breath.

Whereas progressive muscle entails methodically tensing and relaxing diverse/different muscle groups. Just as it is with any other skill, the more the relaxation strategies are done, the more quickly and effectively they work. Other useful relaxation strategies include meditation, massage, yoga, and calm music. However, it is important to note that the aim of relaxation is not to eliminate or avoid anxiety (since anxiety is not completely dangerous) but to make it somehow easier to endure the feelings.

How to Prevent a Relapse

Managing your anxiety disorder effectively is more like an exercise. You continuously need to "keep in shape" as well as making the useful skills a day-to-day habit. However, at times people slide back to old habits, forget and lose the progress they made, and relapse.

A relapse is defined as returning to your old habits and ways of behaving and thinking before you learned the new tactics for overcoming your psychological problem. While it is normal for one to undergo lapses (i.e., a brief return to former habits) over stressful times, fatigue, or low mood, a relapse does not have to occur.

Tips on how to stop lapses and relapses:

The best way to avoid or stop a relapse is to keep practicing CBT skills. If you practice regularly, you will be in good shape to manage whatever circumstances you face.

Tip: *Create your own schedule of the skills you will work on each week.*

First and foremost, figure out when you are susceptible to facing a lapse (e.g., stressful times or change), and you will less likely fall into one. It also helps you create a list of cautionary signs (e.g., regular arguments with family members, more anxious and nervous thoughts) that tell you when your anxiety levels might be on the rise. Once you understand and know your warning signs, you can then create an action plan on how to cope up with them. This involves practicing some CBT techniques like challenging your negative thinking or calm breathing.

Always remember that, like everybody else in the world, you are a work in progress. A better way to stop or prevent future lapses is continuing to work on new challenges. You are less likely to slip back into old ways if you continually work on new or different methods of overcoming anxiety. If you have ever have a lapse, figure out what circumstances led you to it. This helps create a plan for coping with problematic situations or events in the future. Always remember that having lapses occasionally is normal and that you can learn so much from them. How one thinks about their lapse has a big impact on their future behavior. If one thinks he or she is a failure and undoes all their hard work, he/she is more likely to stop trying and end up in a relapse. Instead, it is important to remember that it is difficult to unlearn all the techniques and fall back to square one (i.e., being afraid and anxious and not knowing ways of handling it) since you have already learned the skills of handling your anxiety. In cases where you experience a lapse, it is not the end. You can always get back on track. It can be compared to riding a bike: Once you can ride your bike, it is next to impossible to forget it. You might become a little bit rusty, but it will not take long before you become as good as before.

Keep in mind that having lapses is normal, and they can be overcome. Do not stress yourself or call yourself names such as loser or idiot as it can never help you. Be kind enough to yourself and know that everyone makes mistakes sometimes. Symptom reappearance, setbacks, and relapses are regular. Essentially, if one recovers from an eating disorder, depression, anxiety, OCD, an addiction, or virtually any psychological disorder without any setback, that would be the exception. It is vital to keep in mind that change is not linear. This means that recovering from a psychological, emotional, or behavioral problem rarely goes progressively upward in a straight line. It would be nice if you could get better and better day by day until you achieve full recovery. Unfortunately, that is not how it usually works. And it is okay. Expect the occasional hiccups – forewarned is forearmed. Now that you know setbacks and lapses are normal events and change is not linear, it is an awesome idea to accept the likelihood of lapses rather than live to fear them.

What usually determines the time that a setback/lapse takes is how fast you swing into action to get hold of it. A positive attitude towards overcoming lapses makes a huge difference. That is why it is important to create a relapse prevention plan in case you start to slide back to anxious thoughts or situations. When you feel disheartened, it is easy to discredit all your achievements. Thus, make an accurate and fair assessment of your growth and progress to date. Small changes are very significant.

Lastly, make sure you reward yourself for all the efforts you put in to overcome anxiety. A reward might involve treating yourself by buying a nice meal or a treat. Overcoming and managing anxiety is not always fun or easy, and you definitely deserve a reward for all your hard work and efforts!

Self-Care

Oftentimes, one of the best ways to improve your patience for coping is to make sure that you are providing yourself with the care you need. It is easy to forget to care for yourself when you are so caught up in life, or when you feel as if you are undeserving of basic care.

However, when you are not maintaining yourself, you will not have the patience or energy to handle when life throws you a curveball because you have invested so much of your emotional energy elsewhere. Your emotional battery, so to speak, is either already depleted, or close to being depleted, and you will need to fill it somehow. You are deserving of care, no matter how strongly you feel otherwise; everyone deserves to be able to rest and enjoy themselves sometimes.

What Self-Care Entails

There are plenty of ways you can engage in this self-care, and it will look different for every individual person. The important part is that this self-care works to make you a healthier person in some way, shape, or form.

The self-care also needs to be enjoyable for you; just as when you diet, you want to enjoy your food, you should enjoy the process of becoming a healthier person overall and when engaging in self-care.

There are four major types of self-care that this book will address, and all of them are important to make a person who is overall a healthy individual, not just physically, but mentally as well. You may add other aspects of your life that you desire to provide yourself with self-care in, such as spiritual or work-place, but these will not be addressed in this book.

Remember to follow the pattern of doing something that will make you healthier in those areas of your life, and you will be able to add those categories to your list as well.

Physical Self-Care

Physical self-care involves actions that keep your body healthy and in a condition that allows you to get through your day-to-day obligations.

It is important for you to maintain your body, as it is the only one you have! You have to cherish it and recognize it as valuable, even if that is difficult for you. Some ways you can care for your body include the following:

- Get enough sleep and keep your schedule regular

- Eat primarily healthily

- Take a walk or get some form of exercise daily

- Rest when your body needs it (i.e. you are sick or injured)

- Eat all of your meals when you are hungry

Psychological Self-Care

Psychological self-care includes activities that help you remain level-headed and engaged enough in the world around you to address any challenges that come your way. These are, in a sense, ways you care for yourself that keep you sane.

Just because you cannot see when your mind needs some care the way you can see when your body does, does not give you an excuse to neglect your psychological health. Some ways you can care for your mind include:

- Keep journals
- Ask for advice or guidance from someone you trust or who knows the situation better than you do
- Relax at least once a day
- Leave your work at work and disengage from work responsibilities when you are home (i.e., turn off your work phone and disable work email notifications)
- Get a hobby, and do it regularly

Emotional Self-Care

Emotional self-care is somewhat different from psychological self-care. It involves providing yourself an environment in which you are safe to feel your emotions, no matter how positive or negative. You deserve to feel emotionally supported, and these are some suggestions to ensure that you do:

- Create a gratitude journal
- Do something nice for yourself each day

- Create friendships in which you can speak honestly about how you are doing.

- Find groups of people that enjoy similar hobbies, such as a book club or a hobby sports group local to you

- Seek out support groups if you are recovering from trauma or trying to cope with something difficult

Relationship Self-Care

This type of self-care keeps you maintaining relationships with others. This is about encouraging friendships that you are secure in, and also maintaining positive relationships with coworkers.

On the other hand, it is also about knowing that it is okay to let go of relationships that are toxic to you, or that you do not desire to be in. Some ways to practice relationship self-care include:

- Prioritize the most important relationships above all others, such as with spouses, children, or immediate family.

- Make an effort to be available to those you love on a regular basis

- Set aside time to spend quality time with your loved ones

- Always attend the special events of your loved ones, such as weddings, birthdays, or other important occasions

- Let go of relationships that are toxic to you, and only foster the ones that make you happy or that you feel secure within

Create a Self-Care Plan

Now that you understand the different aspects of your life that require self-care, you are ready to begin planning one. Take a piece of paper and write down the four categories: Physical, Psychological, Emotional, and Relationships. Under each of these categories, you should write at least one way you will engage in self-care, but more is advised. The more ways you engage in self-care, the better condition your body will be in. Make sure that every self-care act you engage in is one that is legitimately enriching to you and that you will enjoy.

Look at the list you have created, and commit it to memory. You want to ensure that you are confident that you will engage in these steps and that you are committed to engaging in them.

Once you have it memorized, tape it up somewhere you will see it regularly. You could type it up onto a sticky note on your computer, or literally tape up the paper on your mirror, so you see it every time you wash your hands or get ready to go somewhere. You want it somewhere that you will regularly see in order to remind you that it is there and encourage you to move forward with the activities. Next, you need to make it a point to engage in these activities regularly. You need to care for your body and mind over time in order to see results. While one day here and there will not completely derail your progress, when you are spending more days not engaging in self-care than you are, you are likely not going to see much of an improvement in your life.

This is an important step to repairing your mental well-being, and you owe it to yourself to ensure you care for yourself, as no one has as much of a vested interest in making sure you are well then you do. After a month, you should stop and reassess your situation. Record how far you have come, and acknowledge areas of your life that have been improved. Just as you will not lose a drastic amount of weight in a month, you will not see huge changes after one month of self-care, but the ones that are there should be noticeable, at least to you.

Remember, these plans and actions may take upwards of a month before they become habits, so you need to remember to be realistic with your expectations. Check again in three months and record your progress. This is when you should start seeing big improvements in your attitude, behaviors, and a general sense of wellness, especially when pairing this self-care with the other methods of CBT.

Remember to remain patient and realistic as you see progress, and keep up with building the habits. It will get easier with time, and you will see results that are worth the effort.

Depression relief through exercise and nutrition

There are exercises and rituals that can be added to your daily routine to use as alternative coping mechanisms, or to simply help clear your mind so that you can become a more rational thinker. Using exercise like running, walking, or going to the gym proves to be beneficial, as well as techniques like yoga and meditation to clear the mind and make room for positive thoughts.

The reason physical activity works so well to relieve stress and depression is that it answers the fight or flight response. Remember that it is the body's natural reaction to raise stress hormones, and provide immediate energy in response to stress or negativity. If the energy created is not used, it balls up and creates anxiety and negative thoughts. Thousands of years ago, that energy would have been used in physical combat or to run away from danger.

These days, stress is typically caused by work and family life, and there is really no physical output in these situations. However, exercising on a regular basis keeps stress hormones like adrenaline at a minimum, and releasing that pent up stress. Depending on your current physical ability, pick a form of exercise that will get your heart rate up. For some this could be a quick walk around the block, for others it could be a mile run.

Whatever your pace, getting out and moving your muscles feels good for your body and your mind. Exercise has been shown to trigger the release of happy hormones like endorphins that automatically boost your mood. If you are feeling particularly stressed, exercises such as boxing or martial arts may give you the extra release of aggression you need to straighten out your negative thoughts.

Exercise is best practiced on a regular basis, meaning on most days of the week. Most health professionals recommend getting at least a half hour of physical activity five times per week for the best health outcomes, which includes reducing the risk for chronic diseases like heart disease and diabetes. However, we make the same recommendations to add to a solid behavioral therapy plan. Plus, it may ease your stress as your improved health will likely keep you from having stressful medical episodes, and their associated medical bills. It's a win-win.

If you are not cleared for aerobic exercise from your doctor, try yoga or Tai Chi. These exercises focus on slow, fluid movements that are less impactful on joints, and keep the heart rate relatively low. They focus more on balance and flexibility rather than cardio and may be a more appropriate exercise for your fitness level. Don't worry, these exercises have similar effects. In fact, these practices have been touted for improving mind-body connections and aid in the process of relaxation and mental clarity.

Yoga can be done just about anywhere. If you are not familiar, consider taking a class at your local gym or yoga studio, or look for video tutorials online to try it at home. Start with a beginner's class, as the more you practice the more difficult the poses become. Surely, you have seen well-rounded yogis doing gravity-defying back bends that would likely land you in the hospital as a beginner. As with any exercise, it is good to push yourself and make forward progress with fitness, but know and practice within your limits.

Proper nutrition also plays an important role in keeping you healthy, mind and body, and it does so in a number of ways. The primary role of good nutrition is getting a well rounded, nutrient rich diet that supports your daily activities.

This means you want to get protein, carbohydrates and healthy fats from a number of sources that also provide a wide variety of essential vitamins and minerals. Vitamins and minerals, while required in small doses, have big jobs in the body. Each has a special function inside every cell in the body. They are part of chemical reactions that keep things running smoothly, including very important work in the brain. Any time one of those vitamins or minerals is missing, it slows down the chemical reactions that power the cells, which hinders overall function in vital organs like the brain.

Many vitamin and mineral deficiencies (or toxicities) have a direct impact on the brain; therefore it is vital that we get a good variety of them in the diet. If you aren't sure whether or not you are getting the nutrients you need, consider taking a simple multi-vitamin that can help supplement your diet, and consult a nutritionist or registered dietitian to help evaluate your diet. Overall, make sure your plate includes lean meats like beef, chicken or eggs, or vegetarian proteins like legumes, seeds, and tofu. Your plate should also have a hearty serving of vegetables, ranging in colors in order to get your vitamins.

Remember the color of a vegetable often indicates its nutrient profile, so sticking to lettuce and green peppers will not be enough to fully fill out your vitamin and mineral quota. You should eat carbohydrates like potatoes and rice sparingly, and should not be the focus of your plate. There is a lot of talk about carbs being an unnecessary nutrient these days, but they are required for an immediate source of energy, so including small amounts at each meal is perfectly fine.

In general, it is a good idea to avoid processed foods and anything with ingredients you can't recognize. Additives and fillers are often chemically based, and end up being more work for your liver and kidneys to filter and flush out. Extra work means extra stress on the body, which can cause the same stress response as a physical danger, just on a lower level. Reducing stress from potentially inflammatory foods is also important. While everyone will react differently to certain foods, be vigilant of potential food allergies and sensitivities. A good indicator of a problem is with your skin and in your GI tract.

If you have unexplained rashes, even minimal ones that are just a few spots, or if you have occasional bouts of indigestion, you may have a food sensitivity.

These things often get ignored because they do not pose a big threat to health or cause immediate distress, but could cause you more harm long term. Your GI tract is the first line of defense for your immune system. As bacteria, toxins or harmful substances enter the lining of your GI tract flushes out the bad things while absorbing nutrients. If a food allergy or sensitivity exists, exposure to the allergen damages the lining of the GI tract, reducing its ability to separate good from bad.

When toxins or bacteria enter the blood stream as they scoot past the GI lining, some of these things get to the brain, causing chemical imbalances and hindering brain performance, often leading to mental health issues. These foreign substances also elicit an immune response, elevating natural stress hormones in the body, which elevates your risk for depression and anxiety. Recent research is beginning to create stronger correlations between underlying food and environmental allergens that cause seemingly unrelated neurological and mental problems, so this is important to take into consideration. Since everyone is different, the only real way to determine if something in your food supply, or something environmental is having an effect on you is to eliminate the exposure.

In the case of food, ask for help with eliminating possible sensitive foods from a qualified professional, like a registered dietitian.

Best Uses for CBT & Beyond

Now you should be fully aware of the broad ranges of treatment that CBT can be used for and how you can quickly establish a variety of treatment options for many of the symptoms listed below:

Anger issues and anger management - CBT is effective because it holds not only thoughts, but behavior and emotions to account. Anger issues can be quickly quelled by teaching mindfulness combined with behavior modification and the suppression of negative thought.

Anxiety problems - there are many different types of anxiety disorders that can be quickly controlled because CBT works on the root causes and triggers of anxiety efficiently.

Panic attacks - panic attacks can actually make a person feel like they might be dying and are very intense. Understanding the root causes of triggers and ways to suppress and eventually eliminate them is of great value to anyone suffering.

Dysfunctional issues - the list is extensive here and CBT can help all kinds of dysfunctional issues especially as they relate to children, teenagers, and adults.

Childhood problems - many people suffer from childhood problems well into adulthood especially when they deal with abusive homes, anxiety related issues and improper nurturing that can occur at the hands of abusive or poor parents. CBT can tackle the core causes and allow a person to deal with this trauma in a powerful and effective way.

Depression - mindfulness training as well as the ability to refocus one's thoughts, feelings and emotions is a powerful tool that CBT offers to people who are suffering from depressive issues. Few therapies have such a high degree of success and depression need not be a lasting disorder.

Addictive issues like drugs & alcohol - the true strength of CBT is expressed in its ability to relieve people of the need for addictive drugs and/or alcohol or even addictive behaviors. Because we combine the complete spectrum of emotions, behavior and thinking, we are able to affect events in a person's life and also to prevent relapses.

Eating disorders - behavior modification along with identification of eating triggers is a powerful tool that CBT can present in any situation. This even includes the addictive personality and how to deal effectively with it and to deprogram these triggers.

Health issues that cause psychological disorders - many people suffer from a variety of health disorders that also can relate to mental health issues, such as obesity. The powerful combination of behavior modification along with the ability to reprogram how we think and then allow us to grow our emotions in a positive manner can help solve many common health issues and allow us to regain control.

Mood swings – can be a form of the depressive disorder, however, mood swings are much more common and are equivalent to issues relating to bipolar disorder. Here, imbalances can be corrected using behavior modification (i.e. diet, meds.) and the focus can be directed to mindful therapy and meditative practices to help control volatile emotions.

Obsessive-compulsive disorder (OCD) - interestingly enough OCD can be controlled through behavior modification and more mindful focuses. Helping someone to reduce the instances of repetitive negative behavior and to focus on growth towards other productive uses of their time is a primary function of CBT.

Phobias of all kinds - exposure therapy along with behavior modification and cognitive therapy come together to quickly eliminate phobias of all kinds. CBT works wonders here because all elements are brought to bear and fears can be made extinct quickly.

Post-traumatic stress disorder - we have also explained in detail how CBT is highly effective at allowing people suffering from PTSD to eventually recover completely and view the events of their trauma in a new light.

Sexual and relationship problems - acceptance therapy as an extension of CBT along with mindfulness can teach people with relationship and sexual disorder problems how to not only cope, but relearn the importance of connecting with their mate.

Sleep problems - as an extension CBT would teach the importance of regular exercise as well as necessary sleep patterns to maintain good health. The importance of regular sleep is inculcated into the person going through the therapy.

Please keep in mind this is only a partial list of some of the top mental health disorders that plague our society that CBT is effective at dealing with. As a therapist or even a layperson, it is up to you to make the proper decisions necessary to determine what aspect of CBT works best for what situation.

As always, competent therapists are necessary especially those trained in CBT to continue moving forward and to use the therapy because it is highly effective, and can be used in the least amount of time necessary to effect the greatest change. Take the opportunity to consider the best extension of CBT therapy for you, your practice and of course your patients.

Chapter 11:
Working on Specifically Anxiety, Negativity, and Stress

Anxiety is a word that is quite common to most people, but funnily enough, not many people can define the word. When you experience a feeling of worry, nervousness, or unease about something, or maybe about the uncertainty of an outcome, then you are anxious. Anxiety in itself is usually a disorder that affects how we feel or behave. This disorder can even cause some physical symptoms. However, if you are facing such an impairment, you don't have to live with it. Anxiety is treatable.

The best approach to take with the aim of treating is to take on some therapy sessions. Cognitive Behavioral Therapy (CBT), Psychotherapy, and Exposure Therapy are some of the therapies one may majorly consider. The thing with these therapies is that they will help you in controlling your anxiety levels and even help you conquer your fears.

Treating Anxiety Disorders

Some may ask the question: "Why should I go through some hectic therapy session just to treat the disorder while I can simply buy medication and achieve the same result in the comfort of my house?"

That can be an excellent way to tackle it, but the problem is that it is only short term. This is because the medication will just eliminate the physical symptoms, leaving behind the underlying causes of your worries and nervousness. Research has shown that therapy is an effective method to tackle anxiety. How? It simply gives you the tools to overcome your fear and teaches you how to use them. Therapies are usually considered long-term by most people. However, this is not the case with CBT-based anxiety therapy.

Surprisingly, within the first eight to ten months, many people are usually okay. The length of these therapies is generally measured by the severity of the disorder, and also the type. There are various types of anxiety disorders like Generalized Anxiety Disorder (GAD), Obsessive Compulsive Disorder (OCD), Panic Disorder, and many more.

It is now also obvious to note that therapy should be tailored to one's specific symptoms. A person suffering from GAD cannot undergo the same therapy session as one suffering from OCD.

As mentioned before, there are various types of anxiety therapies that can be considered. However, the two leading treatments are Cognitive Behavioral Therapy and Exposure Therapy. These therapies can be used alone or be accompanied by other types of treatment. Another thing to note is that these therapies can be done at an individual level or to a group of people who have the same anxiety problems. We are going to cover the CBT part.

Cognitive Behavioral Therapy for Anxiety

Cognitive Behavioral Therapy primarily works to alleviate both negative cognitions, that is, thoughts and beliefs, and also maladaptive behaviors associated with anxiety. CBT seeks to blend the best parts of behavior and cognitive therapies.

As the name suggests, there are two main components to this therapy: Cognitive Therapy and Behavioral

Therapy. Cognitive therapy is the part that involves one's thoughts. This part examines how one's negative thoughts contribute to anxiety. Behavioral treatment, on the other hand, examines one's behavior and reactions when in situations that trigger anxiety. It is important to note that this type of treatment mainly focuses on our thoughts rather than the events.

This is because one's thoughts determine one's feelings. Let's take an event, like that of getting a job somewhere you never thought you would ever be employed. This event can lead to various feelings which are determined by how you think about the situation. For example:

- The thought that you are fortunate to have landed in such a job will make you feel thrilled and jovial.

- The thought that you are not qualified enough for such a high-end job may make you feel undeserving of the opportunity, and this can lead to stress.

The above represents the same situation but two very different feelings that can be achieved by merely how you think.

Generally, for people with anxiety disorders, their decisions are often clouded with negative thoughts that lead to negative emotions of worry, nervousness, or fear. For such people, Cognitive Behavioral Therapy usually comes in handy because it helps them identify and fight these negative thoughts, thereby avoiding negative emotions that cause anxiety.

Thought Challenging in CBT

Thought challenging is a useful technique used in CBT that helps one consider situations from multiple angles, using actual evidence from your life.

It involves challenging one's negative thoughts and replacing them with more positive and realistic opinions.

This technique usually involves three steps. Namely:

1. **Identifying Negative Thoughts**

Anxiety and negative thoughts are a very evil duo that can lead to very severe problems. People with an anxiety disorder tend to perceive things or events more seriously than other people.

For example, a person who fears dogs will consider touching them as life-threatening. Somebody else will view this as safe as long as he or she approaches the dog in a friendly way.

This step can be tough to take because identifying one's fear is not that simple. The only thing, however, that one must ask is what feeling you had when you started feeling anxious.

This is the only sure way to determine your fear.

2. Challenging negative thoughts

Once the fears and the negative thoughts have been identified, the next thing is to test these thoughts. What does this mean? It basically means evaluating the negative thoughts. Why do these thoughts occur naturally to you?

In this stage, one has to question the evidence behind these negative thoughts and also try to identify any unhelpful beliefs that may lead to negative thoughts. A strategy that one may use in challenging these thoughts is by weighing the advantages and disadvantages of worrying or fearing something.

3. Replacing negative thoughts with positive ones

Once you have challenged these negative thoughts, it is now time to replace these negative thoughts with more realistic and positive thoughts. If this proves hard, one may also find some calming thoughts or words that you can say to yourself if you are facing a situation that causes anxiety.

However, replacing negative thoughts with positive ones is usually easier said than done. This is because the negative thoughts are typically due to a long-term belief which needs much courage and time to break. It is for this reason that cognitive behavioral therapy includes practicing on your own at home.

Managing Stress Self-Help

Why is managing one's stress helpful? Stress can have a hold on your life, causing you to be sad and thus less productive.

It affects your emotional equilibrium and also narrows your ability to think correctly and clearly. Effective stress management can, therefore, go a long way towards relieving a huge burden off your shoulders.

How do you determine whether or not you are under stress? There are various thoughts, emotions, physical sensations, and even behaviors that are associated with this form of mental pressure. Some of these include:

THOUGHTS

- I'll never accomplish this.

- It's not fair. Someone should be helping me.

- This is too much for me.

EMOTIONS

- Angry

- Depressed

- Hopeless

- Impatient

PHYSICAL SENSATIONS

A physical sensation is a physical response to stress and is caused by the body's adrenaline response. Some of the physical feelings associated with stress therefore are:

- Breathing faster

- Hot and sweaty

- Restless

- Bowel problems, usually short pains

- Difficulty in concentrating because one's mind is focused elsewhere

- A headache

BEHAVIOR

- Lack of sleep

- Lack of appetite

- One is not able to settle

- Use of drugs or even an increase in their use. For example, if one is used to smoking, there will be an increased tendency to smoke

Making Positive Changes

This is aimed at basically managing one's stress levels. Various steps can be followed to make positive changes. They include:

1.   Identify the sources of stress or the stressors in your life

It's the first step towards making a positive change. This step is not as straightforward as it sounds. Finding the source of chronic stress can be very complicated.

To ease things a bit for you, here are some of the questions that you can ask yourself to identify the cause of stress.

- What makes you stressed?

- Where am I when I get stressed?

- What am I doing when I get stressed?

- Who am I with when I get stressed?

- What change can I make?

Some may notice that there is very little that they can do to change some situations. These tiny things could make the difference you need, so do not hesitate to perform them.

2. Identify the factors that keep the problem going

Once you have identified the sources of your stress, it is now time to identify the factors that keep this problem going.

3. Thinking differently

This step is fundamentally mental. It means that all you have to change is your thinking towards various situations.

To help you improve your thinking, here are some questions that you ought to ask yourself when faced with a particular case:

- What am I reacting to?

- What is it that is going to happen here?

- Is this fact or opinion?

- How helpful is it for me to think this way?

- Is it even worth it?

- Am I overestimating the threat?

- What meaning am I giving to this situation?

- Is there another way of looking at this?

- What advice would I give to someone else in this situation?

- Can I do things differently here?

Once you have asked yourself these questions and answered them frankly, then you will be able to think positively about a situation.

4. Doing things differently

This step will help with reducing both stress and anxiety. Why? During stress, one usually feels as if many demands cannot be achieved with the available resources.

Therefore, doing things differently by maybe considering what applications are most important can help reduce stress levels.

On the other hand, doing things differently can help in reducing anxiety, in that you can now decide to make time for yourself each day to relax or just for fun.

One might also choose to create a healthy balance, in that you have time to work, rest, and do other things that concern you.

Tips to Work on Anxiety, Negative Thinking, and Stress

There are several ways of fighting anxiety, negative thinking, and stress:

1. Understand Your Thinking Style

This step right here is the first step to take to change the negative thoughts that one usually has.

One must understand how they think precisely. Here are some thinking styles that may help you:

- If you tend to believe that when you fail at one thing, then you have failed at everything, then you are a polarized or black and white thinker.

- If you tend to know what people feel about you and why they act the way they do without them saying so, then you are a person that jumps to conclusions.

- If you tend always to expect disaster to strike no matter what, then you are a catastrophizing thinker. This type of thinker always asks the question: "what if?"

2. The Ability to Recognize Thought Distortions

Once you are able to identify your thinking style, one is able thereby to determine whether it is a thought distortion or not. Types of thought distortions are like those given above in the first step.

They include: catastrophizing, making extremely negative predictions, and also making black or white judgments.

3. The Ability to Recognize Rumination

What is rumination? It is a deep or considered thought about something. Typically, when people ruminate, their problem-solving capacity is significantly reduced. Therefore, it is vital for one to recognize this stage during problem-solving and avoid it at all possible costs.

If avoiding ruminating proves to be hard, then the best thing to do when ruminating is to accept that you are having certain thoughts, recognize that they might not be correct, and then allow them to pass in their own mind rather than trying to block them out.

4.   Cope with Criticism

Criticism is one thing that cannot be avoided in life. On the other hand, it can also lead to unnecessary worries if not adequately managed.

Therefore, one must be able to learn how to cope with criticism. CBT can help one acquire the skills needed to deal with criticism. During the therapy session, try to weigh out if the blame is constructive or not before deciding whether you can use it or shun it away.

Always use evidence to your thoughts so that you can make a decision based on factual evidence.

5.   Learn the Art of Mindfulness

Learning this art of mindfulness will help you gain control of your thoughts and emotions. This is because the art teaches one to view one's thoughts and feelings as objects floating past you that you can stop, observe, or even let pass you by. We will cover this as we go on.

6.   The Ability to Talk to Oneself Kindly about Imperfections and Mistakes

The tendency of speaking to yourself harshly in the case of imperfection has shown to be of no importance.

This is because in most cases it leads to rumination, which then leads to vague problem-solving solutions. On the other hand, research has shown that speaking to yourself calmly can increase self-motivation and also make a person feel much better.

7.   Avoiding Thought Stopping

Thought stopping is the complete opposite to mindfulness. This is because it is the act of being on the lookout for any negative thoughts whatsoever and forcing them to be eliminated.

The problem with this act is that the more you stop these thoughts, the more they will surface during problem-solving. Therefore, avoiding such thoughts and embracing mindfulness is a much better way.

8.   Understanding Your Thinking Diary

What are thinking journals? They are tools that can be used to change any negative thoughts. The importance of these thinking diaries is that they help one identify and determine one's negative thinking styles and thus gain a better understanding of how their beliefs affect their emotions. These diaries are essential in a cognitive behavioral treatment plan and must be completed if you want to capture your thoughts. There are more practical's for that before the conclusion.

CONCLUSION

Thanks for downloading this book. It is my earnest desire to see that people are able to build relationships with themselves. There are too many broken people in the world: despite e the advent of the Internet and the wealth of information from technology, there is still not enough knowledge out there to help them heal from their wounds.

Many of us have been rendered cripple emotionally and mentally by the tragedies that we have endured. We have gone from living to just surviving. We were made for more than that. I don't just want to live; instead, I want to thrive and I want these things for all of us! Emotional healing starts from within and there is no surgery as of this moment that can fix that. However, in the face of this seemingly helpless situation, we have been given the power to turn things around for ourselves.

The game changer in all of this is choice. What have you decided to do with your life today? Are you going to sit back and take everything that is being tossed your way? Or are you going to stand up and say "enough?" These are the choices that you are confronted with today, and your answer will determine the rest of your life.

I hope that you find the courage to choose life every day. No matter what the rest of the world has said about you, the simple truth is that you deserve better. And while you may have become isolated in your struggles, know that you are never alone. Millions of people around the world share stories that are similar to your life experiences. And many of them have done more than just survive those experiences.

They have persevered on top. And the remarkable thing about their stories is that these victories they have didn't come by wealth or a change in their circumstances. It was as a result of a change in their attitude. They recognized their power and they acted on it. The change did not happen overnight. And the change did not stop the moment they got their victory. It is a process that happens every day and they thrive in the fullness of it. The best part is that they do not have a monopoly on this.

You can also rebuild from the loss you have experienced and restore relationships that have been damaged. Tragedy and trauma do not have to characterize your life.

Choose instead to characterize those things that have gone wrong. You can transform your life in 21 days and there is no better time to begin this journey than now. For those who have started, I celebrate you in advance. Be consistent, be diligent, and most importantly, be deliberate!

Lightning Source UK Ltd.
Milton Keynes UK
UKHW021221091120
373077UK00018B/1584/J